Randy & Donna —
If you feel this is
worth while —
please share.

Winter
2007

GARDEN PLANET

The Present Phase Change of The Human Species

By

William H. Kötke

authorHOUSE™
1663 Liberty Drive, Suite 200
Bloomington, Indiana 47403
(800) 839-8640
www.AuthorHouse.com

First published by AuthorHouse 01/31/05

ISBN: 1-4208-2389-2 (e)
ISBN: 1-4208-2388-4 (sc)
ISBN: 1-4208-2387-6 (dj)

Library of Congress Control Number: 2005900030

Printed in the United States of America
Bloomington, Indiana

This book is printed on acid-free paper.

DEDICATED TO THOSE WHO ARE

CREATING THE NEW WORLD

TABLE OF CONTENTS

CHAPTER ONE

THE NEW WORLD

A new post-industrial, post-imperial world is forming under our feet. This is a wholistic reality that will serve as the seed pattern for future generations. This new culture represents the "graduation" of the species to maturity and biological legitimacy. This is the exciting direction into which we can all put our creative energies, without reservation. This is an answer to the fading industrial world. The sprouting seed patterns are miniature human communities that are intent on serving most human needs, locally, within their societies. These communities are loosely called eco-villages. These are intentional communities which are pointed toward self-sufficiency. These nascent institutions float on a tide of cultural creation that has been in motion for some fifty years.

The new culture of the post industrial world has intuitively come up out of the masses of us. No powerful group has organized projects to produce it; it is not the result of powerful backroom planners. Since the mid-twentieth century wholistic responses that constitute the framework of the new culture have been created as reactions to the failing institutions of industrial society. We are not inventing new culture from whole cloth. It's basic pieces have already been road tested over several decades. What we do now is to pull all the pieces together and put them on the ground. In this book we will examine the imminent collapse of civilization, and we will outline the sprouts and buds of the new human culture that is arising.

For as many as two million years our species has been incredibly successful on the earth. As primarily forager hunters we traveled in bands of an average of twenty eight people gathering our food with the seasons and living in balance with nature such that we did not eradicate the living world. Obviously, these groups wandering in their traditional, seasonal migration patterns would need to work together to survive. And such it was. Our elders over a vast amount of time counseled the youth to cooperate, work together, be humble, share, and generally de-emphasize the individual in view of the group importance and survival. It is important that we are not admiring our ancient ancestors because of nostalgia or some romantic notions. Rather, we are looking at how they managed to live in balance with the natural world.

At this point in history studying how humans have managed to live in balance with the earth is important to our own survival. We are not concerned, for our present purposes, whether we like their diets, social practices or other factors when looked at through the lens of values of late industrial western culture.

When the cultural inversion occurred from forager/ hunter to agriculture and the beginnings of imperial society, sharing inverted to material accumulation, greed was socially condoned and the living earth was turned into private property. Cooperation was sacrificed to individualism and selfishness. Individual success, wealth and dominance became central values over concern for the group. We might call this the era of "baubles and beads" which saw the human accumulation of "wealth" to extreme degrees. The culture of civilization has accumulated vast "wealth" and massive ability to destroy life through military means but its social institutions are stunted and its psychology is warped. Any human culture that destroys life so wantonly could not be otherwise.

Our next unfoldment as a species will be to graduate from our educational fling with the self-centered, and selfish things that our ancient elders suggested we not do - to legitimacy as a planetary organism. Our species has gone through the matrilineal or feminine cycle and through the male dominated patriarchy; now we stand on the equalization onset of the next phase.

Our new culture must take responsibility for person and planet. By default, because the destruction is so vast and has endured so long, we are now in a position that we must manage an ecological restoration of our planet's life, or we as a species will not be here. Fortunately we as a species are responding to the planetary plight with self-regulating intuitive responses.

These responses encompass most of the important elements of our human existence. Our view of our occupancy of the earth has changed tremendously. We now have the bioregional view. Peter Berg and his publication *Raise the Stakes* was an early leader of this movement.

Bioregionalism views our planet as a "spotted fawn." It is dappled by watersheds. A watershed is the smallest natural form of human social, political, economic, and biological unit. A bioregion on the other hand could be a large watershed such as the Amazon or Colombia River drainages. As a political and social unit it comprises an area which unifies all of the water that falls on it and unifies the inter-related concerns of that place.

Bioregionalists talk of "living in place." This orientation accepts the fact that we really do live on the earth and we live in a certain place with relationship to all of the other living things that exist there. A bioregionalist would ask us about all of the "necessities of life" and where they come from. We would first want to know where our water comes from, where the food comes from and then where the water goes and where the excrement goes. The bioregionalist looks for a lifestyle that produces one's needs from their own watershed or at least bioregion.

The bioregion is the place where the stability of human culture is being created that can supercede the present view of land as a commodity that any industrial person can do with as they want. The history of earth abuse since the beginning of agriculture and imperial culture has been to treat the earth as a commodity. As imperial cultures biologically exhaust each area, they move on to other more pristine areas to continue their extraction of biological fertility in order to support the imperial masses and the projects of their emperors and financial/military elites.

For a hundred centuries, since the beginnings of agriculture this has been an acute problem. It is obvious to us now in the twenty-first century that humans cannot live on the planet unless they can keep it alive. It is well demonstrated that the extractive, commodity culture cannot do this. Commodity culture buys a piece of the earth or takes it by force in imperial conquest and then uses that place, its topsoil, its timber, its mineral resources or whatever exists there that can be turned into a profit in the imperial culture, and then walks away when the source of that "wealth" is exhausted. In contrast, we must create a human culture that can live in stability on the earth in the same bioregion over many generations. In this way humans who have created a secure, self-sufficient, biological basis that cares for the earth and keeps it alive can develop the cultural intelligence to assist the living earth over time. This new human culture is one that increases the life of the earth and lives from that increase rather than the existing pattern that lives from the decline of the life and fertility of the earth. This is a necessity. If humans can't do this they can't live here. If we cannot become biologically legitimate organisms we're not going to make it on this planet.

The exciting part is that we are creating a culture that is at home in its place on the earth. In general, life looks out for its progeny. Birds raise their young and try to give them the best chance for life. Plants use all kinds of sophisticated strategies to give their seeds the best chance but the humans organized into imperial/industrial culture have little sense of preserving life for their offspring or, seemingly, even caring about the progeny. Our new cultural creation will return us to that capacity of thinking toward the seventh generation.

We are creating a new culture that humans, except in small groups in isolated times and places, have not known. We have graduated from the monkey level where we collect bright objects and indulge in the primitive politics of who gets to be the alpha in the herd. We are creating a society of human maturity that serves each member of the society rather than being organized for the benefit of the patriarchal elites. This is a culture that facilitates self actualization and human development.

This new culture which is manifesting, will be described in the following chapters. It is one in which the material world is stabilized and cultivated and progress is measured by human development and genius in the non material realms - not material growth. To have a culture that serves the growth of the human potential of each person is true wealth, and we shall have it. We have already created basic elements of the new culture in methods of healing, food growing, diet, spirituality, government, social institutions and new and creative ways of social interaction. We also now have planetary communications systems which can aid us immensely. We should not hold the image that civilization will suddenly disappear; there will be many elements of it that will be helpful as it declines. We can hold the image that the seeds that are sprouting within the composting mass are the seeds of reality for the new human species.

For several million years we humans have been governed by our cultural conditioning. When we depended on inherited culture, and had questions, we asked the elders.

They had lived longer than us, and chances were good that they would have an answer. We lived by the traditions of our culture, and we perceived reality through that cultural lens. We no longer live in a culture that teaches respect for elders; now twelve-year olds have to teach the elders how to program a VCR. In a rapidly changing technological society it is the young who are most informed about the industrially produced environment. In important ways we have no culture, except that existing in libraries and video stores. Now society, especially in "advanced" industrial countries, is held together administratively more than by the social values. Our lives are conditioned, informed, and controlled, by mass social institutions over which we as individuals have little or no control.

This is not to say that we should eschew knowledge from the past that could be useful for us in the future. This is to say that it is the cultural values of civilization that are creating the planetary suicide. It is these that we cannot take into the future.

In a sense we have been liberated from human culture. Now we talk of choosing lifestyles, and this is real. We now are liberated enough to conceive of creating a new human culture.

But, to find our way, we must put it all together, and we must overcome tremendous challenges to reach the prize. We walk through a planetary mine field of conflict and disturbance to reach this end, and we will be living it in community and creating it while we walk.

CIVILIZED HUMANS ARE KILLING THE EARTH

The human problem is that civilized humans are killing the life on the earth in small and large increments. Inasmuch as the humans survive by expropriating from the life of the earth, we are killing that which feeds us and cannot, for long, endure. This book is about that conundrum

This human problem is the product of the ten-thousand-year-old culture/society termed "civilization." This human culture can also be described as a culture of empire in view of its eight to ten thousand year history stretching from the Sumerian empire of ancient times to the British/ U.S. empire of present day. The social configuration involves an emperor surrounded by a small class of military/financial individuals and other key people in the management of the empire. This class of people then rests upon and receives the "profits"of the productive and controlled masses under them. Historically much of this controlled mass were slaves (e.g., the Jews in Babylon or Greek and Roman cities where often over half the population were slaves and in the present-workers often resemble wage slaves).

The shape of present industrial society is little different than its ancestor-Babylon. In the present U.S., one percent of the population owns some eighty percent of the wealth of the country. Various economists give somewhat different numbers of this configuration, but generally what it describes is imperial human culture functioning, structurally, in a manner very similar to Babylon. The words are different but the basic framework of the society is the same, with the same purpose-growth of material wealth and social power for both the elites and the emulating subjugates. In the present, one important way that the ruling elite support the emperor is by paying hundreds of millions of dollars for political campaigns and political control.

This human culture, which began with agriculture and herding in Central Asia and in Northern China, is the problem. It is killing the life of the earth. At the present time it is a culture with an exponentially expanding population, with growing material consumption, based upon dwindling resources and a dying planet.

As material resources become exhausted and we come into the post-industrial world, what we humans become--the personal, social and bioregional, shapes that we form-will be the seed pattern imprinted for the next grand cycle.

We have time constraints. Everything in our life-on-earth- reality is in dynamic motion. Important forces are in exponential rates of expansion (a veritable explosion). Exponential seems only a word. Its reality can be apprehended when one considers that the earth lost twenty percent of its topsoil between 1975 and 2000 and will lose twenty percent

2000 to 2025, or the understanding that nearly half of the arctic ice cap has melted-then the realization of this type of swift progression is possible-in meaningful terms.

PLANETARY CONSCIOUSNESS BY DEFAULT

We have now come to the point of planetary consciousness by default, when the climate threatens to change and alter our food supply system, or we worry about skin cancer because of ozone depletion, or the ocean levels rise and threaten port cities. From local consciousness, we are forced to elevate our view to planetary conditions and assume planetary consciousness. In the same manner, if one is making long range plans, here in the beginning of the Twenty-First Century, one must adopt a planetary view. Climate-change, in itself, promotes this. We would want to know how much longer corn and beans are going to grow in the place where we live. If we are dry-land farmers, we would be interested in the question of flood/drought.

Our window of opportunity for creative effort will only be open for a few short years before we are engulfed by the turmoil of the future.

The leaders of civilization are not going to tell us that they are captains of sinking ships. They are not going to tell us that they have led us into a trap with no exit. For us to learn the reality and to forge a response, we will need to be supported by all of the useful information that we can muster. If we individually, intend to survive creatively, we can't shirk the responsibility for our own lives. We will need to look at some very distasteful facts and analyses. This is not the time to dismiss negative realities; understanding them aids us in creating positive responses. If we expect to be part of the solution and to be conscious in the here and now, we must cease emotionally identifying with the movie and begin to look these facts in the eye and analyze how they came to be. If we can't thoroughly examine our situation without having an emotional collapse then maybe we are not going to make it. We must ask what it is about the dynamics of our culture that has brought us to this point so that our responses in the future do not become merely a reflection of the past. This is a very important point. There are people who have little information and no analysis who feel that recycling their tin cans and planting a tree or two will substantially solve the "environmental problem."

The cynics, the already defeated, the unfortunate injured who exist in negative emotional states, will deny and resist the idea that humans can create utopia, whereas demonstrably, humans can create satisfying and creative cultures. There are numerous (though not well known) examples in history of such societies. One common characteristic of these cultures is that they were and are integrated with and adapted to the energy flows of life on earth.

THE CHALLENGE WE FACE

I invite you to come with me and examine the basic question of our age, a question common to each one of us. The question that we all share is the continuance of our species on the planet earth. This is "the big story" of our time. Many trends of history are culminating in this era and at this pivot point in history great and profound changes are occurring. This offers us the possibility of great opportunity, as well as great tragedy. We exist at a pivot point of history in which Industrial Civilization is exhausting and a new configuration and substance of human society is forming.

FACING THE ULTIMATE - THE NUCLEAR THREAT

At this point, looking down through the centuries, the prospect for industrial society does not look good. On the extreme end of threat we have the stockpile of nuclear weapons pointed at us. The nuclear powers have enough operational nuclear weapons in missiles, bombs and such to basically wipe the life off this planet. At the dawn of the New Century we find the two nuclear superpowers still in confrontational posture. The U.S., as of this writing, has 3,000 submarine based missiles pointed at Russia and the Russians reportedly have 2,800 missiles pointed at the U.S. In such an exchange the blasts would do much damage but then the survivors would sit under a global nuclear winter cloud for years after. According to scientific assessment the blasts would throw up such a horrific cloud of debris that the clouds would encircle the planet and block out the sun for years. Sitting under this prolonged radioactive cloud, life would have little chance.

Not as dramatic but extremely sinister is the fact that today wars fought by the industrial nations are nuclear wars inherently, because of the use of depleted uranium weapons. Scientists have discovered a process of turning nuclear waste, specifically Uranium 238, into one of the hardest, densest metals known. These shells, bombs and missiles can travel right through steel, as if it were hot butter. This weapon is just too good for the militarists to turn down. When this metal hits a tank for example, it vaporizes. As it vaporizes and mixes with the dust and smoke the toxic radiation is released for a life span of tens of thousands of years to blow around the surface of the planet and threaten the life of anyone who inhales a particle. Scientists in India have calculated that the DU radiation released in Iraq in the second invasion by the U.S., is equivalent of two hundred and sixty-nine Hiroshima sized nuclear bombs. DU weapons were used in the Balkans wars, in Afghanistan, and at military firing ranges such as Vieges island in Puerto Rico, Guam and other firing ranges around the world.

THE THREATS PROLIFERATE

We have enough nuclear weapons to obliterate the life of the planet. From this extreme of destruction, we then turn to other large- scale, self-inflicted, events such as deforestation, desertification, soil exhaustion, erosion, and poisoning; planet heating and climate change, ozone layer destruction, the elimination of ocean fish stocks, mineral resource exhaustion, petroleum exhaustion, natural gas exhaustion and so forth. The culture popularly termed civilization has caused the third mass die-off of species on the planet: we are losing bio-diversity.

The outright killing of species such as the Passenger Pigeon and the destruction of living habitats has caused the largest extinction of species since the era of the die-off of the dinosaurs and other species sixty million years ago and the number of species disappearing now, increases each year. After living very successfully on the earth for several million years, the human species is also ultimately facing mass die-off, after only ten thousand years of adopting agriculture and developing the culture called civilization.

Global Warming

A secret study done by the Pentagon and recently obtained by the media, envisions England with a Siberian climate by 2020. Massive world-wide instability will ensue after food supplies decline, mega-droughts begin, and military conflicts break out in resource wars for food, water and energy.

Planetary heating is causing glaciers to melt in high mountains all over the earth. Recently an ancient mummified man (termed the "Ice Man") was found intact high in the Alps. He was found because the ice that had encased him for so long had melted. Archaeologists and scholars in Peru have made new discoveries of mummified bodies on high mountain tops for the same reason. Huge ice shelves have been breaking off of Antarctica in recent years and some forty percent of the arctic ice mass has melted. Scientist are studying the shifts of climate. In one European study they examined a timed system where the oak trees budded out in the spring, a particular species of moth laid eggs on the oak so that the young would have oak buds to eat and then a species of north migrating birds came through and feasted on the moth larvae. Now, the oaks bud out ten days earlier, the moths miss the buds and the traveling birds can't have lunch when they stop over. This kind of shredding of ecosystems is what we will be facing in the future - in spades.

Severe weather events are increasing as warming progresses. Economic losses from these events in the 1990's were triple the amount in the 1980's, five times that of the 1970's, and eight times the losses in the 1960's.

The most dire consequence to humans will be the decline of food supply. Crops are grown in various places because of the local climate. They need rains at certain times and sun at certain times and an accustomed temperature regime. When these elements do not exist, the food supply system collapses.

The U.S. Pentagon study suggests that dramatic climate change could take place in just a few years (less than ten). Ice core samples indicate that abrupt climate changes have happened in the past. They point at one example at the end of the ice age 13,000 years ago. Temperature had risen in Greenland to near what it is now and then suddenly plunged and reverted to ice age conditions for 1,300 years. Much evidence points to the shut down of the "conveyor." This North Atlantic Current brings warm water up from the south along the Atlantic seaboard. It then sweeps north and toward Europe. With the rush of fresh water from the melting arctic ice, however, this climate-controlling current is breaking up due to excess fresh water floating over heavier salt water. This stops the benefit of the current and freezes Europe. In the last of these occurrences, icebergs appeared as far south as Portugal. Temperatures fell as far as five degrees in some parts of North America and Asia and six degrees in Europe. In northern Europe precipitation dropped nearly thirty percent. Drought and floods occurred with violent storms and high winds. Due to their study the Pentagon sees this as a national security issue with societies, at least in the Northern Hemisphere, in turmoil.

The Dying Oceans

Half a century ago, Thor Heyerdhal and Jacques Cousteau both warned of the massive litter of plastics and oil slicks in the world's oceans. Since then more monitoring of the dying oceans has been done. It has been discovered that coral reefs are disappearing fast. Ten percent are gone and seventy percent will be gone in forty years if the destruction continues. Coral reefs are the ecological environment of over one quarter of ocean plant and animal species and important incubators for more open-ocean fish species. One of the culprits is global warming which is changing the temperature for these fragile beings, and the rising levels of carbon dioxide accompanied by rising acidity in the oceans is inhibiting the corals' ability to make their skeletal limestone. Another contributor to coral death is the wiping out of mangrove swamps world wide which themselves are important ocean incubators. Heretofore, the swamps filtered runoff water and sequestered toxins before they reached the coral reefs. Other destruction comes about from the usual destructive human shoreline activities such as fishing with dynamite, fishing with poisons, sewage runoff, farm runoff, petroleum pollution and so forth.

Because of over-fishing and ecological disruption, recent information indicates that all of the 17 major ocean fisheries were being harvested at or beyond sustainable levels and that nine of these fisheries are collapsing. The species crashes of ocean fish stocks has been happening since 1935, and the tempo has increased over time. In 1935 the Antarctic Blue Whale population crashed, 1945 - East Asian Sardines, 1946 - California Sardines, 1950 - Northwest Pacific Salmon, 1961 - Atlantic-Scandian Herring, 1962 - Barents Sea Cod, 1962 - Antarctic Fin Whale, 1972 - Peruvian Anchovy. Since 1972, species stocks have collapsed even more rapidly.

Ocean phytoplankton produce some seventy percent of the world's oxygen. Pollution kills phytoplankton and the increasing ultraviolet light resulting from ozone layer weakening, also kills phytoplankton. Phytoplankton is a basic species at the bottom of the ocean food chain, so all ocean species are threatened by this.

Areas of ecological sinks are now occurring in the oceans, particularly near shores. These sinks are created by toxic pollution and by runoff of farm fertilizers and sewerage which energizes the ocean ecosystem causing algae blooms which use up the oxygen so that all oxygen users die. Dead areas in the oceans include the Golden Horn Estuary of Turkey, areas all through the Mediterranean, areas off the coast of Europe and the same in North America. One North American dead zone extends from the mouth of the Mississippi, three hundred miles into the Gulf. This lifeless zone is ten miles wide.

The Vanishing Soils

Topsoil, which is the basis of much life on earth, is disappearing with increasing rapidity. Researchers calculate that we lost one fifth of the planet's arable land between 1975 and 2000. We will lose at least that much between 2000 and 2025. In Iowa, it costs five bushels of topsoil for each bushel of corn grown. Soil abuse comes about by compaction, exhaustion, erosion, and poisoning with toxic chemicals. Researchers say that an estimated 36 percent of world cropland is declining in productivity because of soil erosion.

Much soil abuse is connected to farming and grazing. Overgrazing and the resulting ecological decline, combined with consequent soil erosion, has been rampant since Babylon and the Chinese Empires. The soil ecological community depends on a healthy overlying ecosystem which drops organic debris to it, which is "eaten" by the "decomposers" within the soil community. If the plants are stripped from the earth by herders, the soil starves. The soil must be fed in order to produce nutrient for the plants standing on it. One ton of beef represents the depletion of 26 pounds of calcium, 54 pounds of nitrogen, 3 pounds of potassium, 15 pounds of phosphorus and many trace elements. All of this comes from the soil and the plants growing on it.

Desertification

The total drylands of the world are 7.9 billion acres. Ten thousand years ago, before the arrival of the civilized, these acres were covered by healthy arid or semi-arid ecosystems. Now sixty one percent of these acres are degraded and desertified. The desertification generally is caused by overgrazing but firewood collection and clearing land for the plow also contribute. There are areas also in which forests have been cleared for the plow, soil fertility then exhausted, and then grazing follows on what little grass and tough, thorny bushes grow there. In North America forty percent of drylands are desertified. Desertification is more rampant in Asia and Africa. In Iran for example, sand dunes have covered 124 villages, and in neighboring Afghanistan nearly 100 villages have been buried. On a larger scale, we find that major deserts in Eastern Central Asia and stretching into Northern China are merging into huge continental deserts. Millions of acres a year disappear from ecological health into this category with increasing rapidity.

Deforestation

Forests have been an energy source for civilization since it began. When they aren't being cleared to get at their rich soils they are depleted for firewood, building materials, and a factor that has consumed much forest in the past, the smelting of metals.

About forty percent of the land area of the earth was forested prior to civilization. Now about a tenth of that remains (94 billion acres to 9.9 billion). The world's forests decline at over 100 million acres a year. As population and industrial production rises this number increases rapidly. If the present rate of destruction of tropical rain forests continues *without* increase, researchers state that it will all be gone by 2050, but of course like other dynamics of modern life the forest is going down with increasing rapidity.

Global Warming is factoring into this equation also. In addition to acid rain, rising temperatures change environments of the trees and produce stress which then makes the forest vulnerable to bugs and diseases.

The countries of the Third World are losing forest at the rate of an area the size of Kansas each year. In the Industrial Countries, forests are slightly gaining but much of this is due to replanting after logging which means that one industrially valuable tree species is alone planted. A forest is a vast complex organism with many species participating. To call a tree plantation a forest is a joke, but professionals have included these areas in their numbers as well as areas that are not closed canopy forests. The FAO notes that only forty percent of what researchers calculate as forest in the above summaries are actually large, closed-canopy, frontier forests that are large enough to contain all of their wide-ranging species.

Water

The question of planetary water is very serious. Agriculture uses some 70 percent of human used water. As it requires 1,000 tons of water to produce 1 ton of wheat, many wheat importing countries that are often also water deficit countries, really, are also importing water. Each gallon of water can produce profits for agriculture, but industrial uses of that gallon are much more profitable. Consequently, we find planet-wide that industrialization outbids agriculture for water.

Unseen water tables underground are real sleepers in the water question. They are being both rapidly depleted and rapidly contaminated. A small example is Sacramento, California where military bases and an Inter Continental Ballistics Missile factory have polluted the underground waters with perchlorate. This toxin is associated with thyroid damage that causes metabolic and hormone disruption and also cancer. It is associated with impaired brain development and bone development in fetuses. It is linked to reduced IQ's, mental retardation, loss of hearing or speech, deficits in motor skills, learning disorders and ADD.

In the same way that other aquifers are polluted, the substance forms an underground plume from where it was dumped. Numerous wells have been drilled which are pumped in order to track the plumes so that the contaminated water is not used. These plumes pollute an ever widening area and thereby severely restrict the amount of ground water that can be used. The point here is that pollution of underground waters is happening all over the industrial world, but it is technical and out of sight (so little notice is taken that substantial waters under our feet are being polluted) and consequently ever increasing portions of it is being withdrawn from human use.

The outright depletion of groundwaters is taking place in many areas of the world. The most severe depletion is East Asia, Central and South Asia, the Mid-East, North Africa, part of Europe and many parts of the United States. A number of countries who are trying to outrace population expansion are overpumping and depleting ground water in order to attempt to maintain or increase grain production. This bubble of course will burst and leave, then, a bloated population sitting on top of exhausted aquifers with little to eat. In Beijing, China for example, wells are now one-half-mile deep. Major grain producers-Northern China, much of India, the U.S., and the country of Pakistan-are headed in this direction of aquifer depletion.

In order to image the massive planetary withdrawal of underground water, researchers conclude that the water pumping already done in the High Plains (Ogallala) aquifer, the Pheonix -Tuscon basin, and the Central California Valley in the U.S., would be equivalent to about 1.3 mm of sea level rise world-wide.

The country of Pakistan is projected to add 200 million people to its population by 2050. Yet, its grain production is affected by falling water tables. Water tables near Islamabad are dropping one to two meters per year, and near Quetta, three and one half meters per year.

When underground waters are depleted, the rivers above them often run dry. This happens because the rivers are riding at the top of the ground water. When rivers run dry ecologies die. Big rivers also die. Major rivers of the earth that do not now, or only periodically do reach the ocean are: the Colorado, U.S.A., the Amu Darya in Central Asia (does not reach the Aral Sea which is going dry), and the Yellow River, China. The Nile, Indus and Ganges are only a trickle when they reach the ocean. Most other big rivers are greatly overtaxed with pollution and upstream withdrawals that threaten the ecological integrity of the region.

Irrigation supports forty percent of the planet's food. Irrigation is often only a short term solution. Salinization and water-logging often take irrigated land out of production. Russian soil scientists estimate that 60 to 80 percent of irrigated lands of the earth will ultimately be ruined. Now, an estimated two-hundred to three-hundred thousand irrigated hectares pass out of cultivation each year out of a total of over two hundred million hectares being irrigated.

Irrigation is often associated with dams. Surface evaporation from dams and canals in semi-arid desert environments averages around fifty percent. Dams themselves are only short term solutions. All dams will eventually silt up depending on the disturbance and destruction of their watersheds. Some dams in very abused watersheds only last twenty to thirty years, but others may go several hundred.

Species Extinction

It just makes common moral sense to a mature human that it is not right for humans to drive to extinction a being, a life form, that has been on this planet for millions of years. To the morally impaired, the argument is often made that extinct species could have benefitted humans. We could have found new drugs in extinct rainforest species, we could have used certain species to produce valuable products; and of course these observations are correct. Species extinction also shreds ecosystems, and we humans are dependent on them. Biologists state that each species is related, through the ecological energy flow system, including the food chain, to an average of ten to thirty other species.

The extinct dodo bird explains this. The bird lived on the Mauritius Islands in the Indian Ocean and ate the fruit of the Calvaria tree. The tree fed the dodo and the bird transported its seeds. It was necessary for the heavily coated seeds to pass through the acid bath of the dodo's intestinal system in order to germinate. No Calvaria tree has germinated for three hundred years since the last dodo died.

During this civilized, eye-blink of human history, of ten thousand years, species are increasingly driven to extinction by outright killing and habitat destruction. This instant in history when looked at in geological time frames, is seeing maybe the second largest extinction of species since life began, all attributable to humans in the culture of civilization.

Europe which has long hosted the civilized and industrial culture is hard hit. In France, 57 percent of the remaining mammal species are threatened with extinction as well as 58 percent of the remaining bird species, 39 percent of the reptile species, 53 percent of the amphibian species, and 27 percent of the fish species. The auroch, the European wild ox is extinct. The last one died in 1627. Extinction is forever.

Planet wide, 24 percent of mammal species are threatened with extinction, 12 percent of birds, 25 percent of reptiles, 21 percent of amphibians, 30 percent of fishes, 29 percent of invertebrates, and 49 percent of plant species.

Food Production

Food is now a critical world issue. The world's per capita grain harvest is slowing down, the water tables are dropping, and the climate is doing unpredictable things. Over one hundred countries import some of the grain that they use and 40 import rice. Some import small percentages of their use others close to 90 percent. China, with falling water tables, failing agricultural experiments in it drylands regions and exploding population, is about to come on the world market for grain. As China begins to exceed its food self-sufficiency this will have a great impact on food availability and prices. Food is <u>*not*</u> grown to feed hungry people; it is grown to make profits. Soon only the wealthy will be able to bid for adequate supplies. At this point already, it is estimated that 40 million people die each year from hunger-related diseases.

<u>Energy Exhaustion</u>

Firewood as an energy source is an extreme problem in our deforested world. As forests decline around villages and cities in the Third Wold, people have to travel farther and farther to find fuel to cook food for the day. The overarching problem of course is the world petroleum supply. Richard Heinberg states in his definitive work, *The Party's Over; Oil, War and the Fate Of Industrial Societies* that the planetary petroleum supply will peak production in 2006 (plus or minus a few years).

As almost everything in industrial society has an energy input, it is not difficult to see what will happen when petroleum prices begin to skyrocket. Unless immediate changes in world social policies are made, there will be a mass die-off of humans. One basic problem is that humans are "eating petroleum." Half of the world's people eat because of the added production of food caused by injecting artificial fertilizer into essentially "farmed out" soils. This energy trade-off began after World War I and accelerated after World War II. If industrial agriculture does not have artificial fertilizers which are developed from petroleum and petroleum energy, a mass die-off will occur.

The Human Population Disaster

Many people in the U.S. become agitated with the spill-over of population from Mexico. However, we need a broader perspective to understand that the population doubling time of Mexico is 22.5 years and that many other Third World countries are adding population at or near this level. This of course is in sharp contrast with the remaining populations of forager/hunters who are not now, nor have they ever been subject to the kind of massive population explosion experienced by the civilized. Immigration from Mexico is only a very small part of a massive phenomenon that will not be fixed by simply stopping immigration from Mexico to the U.S..

As we expand into the future, the numbers of landless and homeless will be swelling and the masses of moving people will get larger. This is exacerbated by the pyramidal structure of imperial culture and the question of who owns the land. World-wide, there are now an estimated thirty six million refugees, both external, who have left their country and internal, within the country. A significant percentage of these people are ecological refugees escaping drought, deforestation, soil exhaustion and such. Many others are fleeing from resource wars and land wars. As these numbers of landless swell, we look at who controls land and what the trajectory of this situation might be. In the U.S., 3 percent of the population owns 95 percent of the privately held land. A U.N. study that looked at 83 countries, concluded that less than 5 percent of rural landowners control three quarters of the land. Some examples are: 86 percent of South Africa is owned by the white minority, 60 percent of El Salvador is owned by the richest 2 percent, 80 percent of Pakistan is owned by 3 percent, 74 percent of Great Britain is owned by 2 percent, and 84 percent of the private land in Scotland is owned by the richest 7 percent of the population.

Many have seen the terrifying population numbers, but far fewer see the additional stress from landlessness. As Globalization continues to funnel wealth to the top and impoverish those below in the pyramid, we are heading toward massive disaster with multitudes of our species wandering over the earth with no legal place to be, as nearly every inch of the earth's surface now is owned by someone or some government. Food is produced for profit; water is sold for profit; and land is held for profit; the masses of the poor will get none unless they pay.

THE BLIND ALLEY

The system of short term gain and long term loss, which we call industrial society, is thoroughly trapped in its final throes. A key principle of ecology is that one cannot do only one thing. That is, each action always has more than one consequence. A seminal study was done in the 1960's which shows this clearly. This is the study titled *Limits To Growth*, done by Donella and Dennis Meadows, and others, under the auspices of the *Club of Rome*. The *Club* invited many dozens of scientists to work with them on an effort they called Project On The Predicament of Mankind.

The scientists put statistical information from each of their specialties on a huge mainframe computer and then began extrapolating to see where our future is headed. We live in a material culture where all the barrels of oil, acres of wheat observed by satellite, acres of Amazonian forest disappearing, numbers of humans, and many other quantifiable changes can be calculated. As these numbers move, they can be tracked. This is where we identify with numbers the exponentially exploding population with growing material consumption based on dwindling resources and a dying planet.

The human culture of empire, which began in Northern China, the Indus Valley empire, and along the Tigris-Euphrates river system, is a specific kind of human culture that has specific cultural values that create the phenomenon of growth. Growth is the "reason to be" of imperial culture. In the present industrial system growth is essential. Grow or die is the watchword of financiers and CEO's. The paying of interest on money is one of the basic dynamics. Every CEO must grow their company and its dividends at a higher percentage of growth than the interest rate or the capitalists will simply sell their shares and put the money in a bank. In another dynamic we see that the food supply must expand in order to feed the exponentially expanding human population. The *Club* scientists examined the basic five dynamics of our industrial world. These are human population, agricultural production, natural resources, industrial production, and pollution.

The scientists put their numbers on the mainframe computer and extrapolated them into the future. First, they assumed a stable, zero growth population. They found that wealth would increase along with industrial production which resulted in exhaustion of resources resulting in a die-off. When they assumed unlimited resources and energy they found that the world became choked with toxic pollution (and asthma/cancer type illness) from the acceleration of industrial production added to a continuing population explosion, resulting in the eventual die-off. This is where the aficionados of "free energy" are. In their desperation to keep industrial civilization going they would simply charge up the system with more production, pollution, and population.

Resources are depleted, toxics become manifold, population massive- then the die-off.

The industrial system is trapped within these interactive dynamics. The authors of this report state that: "The basic behavior mode of the world system is exponential growth of population and capital followed by collapse." Extrapolating their global model, the scientists found that the present system could not go much farther than 2020 before collapse. This of course is computer modeling that considers these five dynamic factors and not, say, world war, an asteroid hitting or any other event.

Although this study was exemplary in an academic sense and sponsored by a group of concerned "world leaders," it never received much coverage from the corporate media or other institutions. Little children can understand that we can't have an exploding population based on dwindling resources, forever. Yet those in power are in power because of the existing system, and they are not going to acknowledge that it will not provide for our progeny and other living things.

IS THERE ANY HOPE?

No, there is no hope for civilization and its industrial society. An exponentially exploding human population, with growing material consumption, based on dwindling resources and a dying planet, won't work! If we try to hang on to the shopping mall and push-button living, there is no hope. Humans, unaware of alternatives, will defend their way of life as a matter of survival. They will tinker, finesse, duck and dodge trying to keep the expiring beast alive. In fact the predatory beast is one of the most destructive things ever to hit this planet. The record of slavery; female suppression through patriarchy; the denial of spirituality through the use, by the powerful, of institutional, hierarchal, and elite dominated religion; thousands of years of continual warfare caused by military based cultures of empire, and the swift die-back of the life of the earth should be enough to indicate to us that we need to look somewhere else for a standard of behavior.

The hubris of the cultivated intellect in civilized society indicates to the involved humans that they can and should fix it. Now that the civilized have eaten up and grown fat on the earth, they wish someone to bring the miraculous solution to fix the situation, so that they will not have to make any uncomfortable changes in themselves or their lives.

Civilization is coming to an end, but there is no reason that we should play starring roles in that movie. There are millions of war refugees on the earth, there are millions of environmental refugees, there are many starving and many in the Third World who truly have nothing to hope for. For them, the end of the world has already begun: it just has not yet reached the population centers of imperial power.

Yes, humans could fix it, but the history of civilization suggests that they will play out the game to the end. There will be a mass die-off. Meanwhile the movie that we are starring in is called "Creating a New World." We can now choose a life-style reality.

This will be the heroic effort of visionaries. We can do it. Many are far down the trail, bending toward it. Humans have powerful creative abilities and can easily do these things. In fact if all the humans on the earth now were able to see the whole picture at the same time and take action the situation could be handled over the whole earth even now. But, until this occurs, we will be moving forward into our future.

Foremost, we must establish biological legitimacy on this planet. Hence, we must be able to put a human culture in place for many generations so that we can develop the cultural knowledge of how to keep the living planet alive. This is the focus of the next chapter. The initial step is to plant the new seed on the earth. In this next chapter we will review proven techniques already in operation that will allow our communities to grow more food per acre than industrial agriculture while actually building soil and restoring the ecology. This alternative will allow us to also include endangered species and thereby help us save bio-diversity.

CHAPTER TWO

THE BIOREGIONAL PERMACULTURE

THE QUESTION OF BIOLOGICAL LEGITIMACY

Our effort to place ourselves on the planet with biological legitimacy is central to the question of our being here as a species. After our experience of being conditioned by the mechanical world we must learn to relate to living things. All living things have a metabolism. That is, they are energy flow systems. They consume and excrete energy. Everything is food and everything is excrement. Even the planet practices this cyclic behavior as lava boils out of volcanos to cover the surface and sheets of the surface submerge under tectonic plates. Cosmically, supernovas explode and become black holes. Our effort will be to maximize the metabolism of our bioregion and watershed. This is the health of our place.

Biological diversity is the path to ecosystem health. The ecosystem builds toward the climax stage, such as an old growth forest. Prior to civilization most of the planet was climax ecosystem. The climax ecosystem contains the highest number of species and produces the most photosynthesis per acre. As the ecosystem builds in diversity more species fill more niches to increase photo synthetic efficiency and build biomass. The climax ecosystem, held in dynamic equilibrium, is the standard of health of the planet.

But, as we look around us we find that the forests are gone, the prairies are gone, and some rivers have disappeared. What has happened? Civilization has happened. Let's look at our million year culture as forager hunters. We simply lived eating the fruits of the earth. We were imbedded in the ecological energy flows of the earth. Finally, some of our species made the symbolic decision that we were not satisfied with what the earth provides. We would use our intellectual function to force the earth to produce more.

THE RELATIONSHIP OF THE CULTURE OF EMPIRE TO THE EARTH

We stopped moving. We created houses and villages around eight thousand years in the past. This is *civis*, living in houses and villages, the root word of civilization. In the matriarchal phase we flowed with the planet's energy. Symbolically, the fire belonged to the woman. The woman stayed in the center of the camp by the fire and protected the children. The man ranged the periphery guarding against intrusion. The woman went out to gather plant foods, the man ranged farther hunting animals. In the camp the woman was the most productively powerful. She usually tanned the hides, made the clothes and performed many other tasks which were indispensable in the continuation of a cooperative group. She also gathered the plant food which was usually available as a food base even if the man could not find an animal to eat.

We see this pattern in the Six Nations Iroquois Confederacy (Hau de no sau nee) of the North-Eastern U.S. After the men make the big talk in council their decision is passed to the Clan Mothers for approval or disapproval. The women have power in those tribes because they do the most to keep the family going and are the center of it.

CREATION OF THE PATRIARCHY

When we stopped moving with *civis*, in the patriarchal cycle, the dynamics changed. We stopped, built habitation and began to collect material goods. At this point we switched to a different energy system. We began agriculture, making us dependent on the topsoil. In Central Asia, an important origin point of civilization, we domesticated wheat and barley. Annual plants, especially those that have become human selected, grow rapidly and have the ability to suck up soil fertility quickly. This is an important reason why row-crop agriculture is based on annual plants and why they exhaust the soil so rapidly.

Civis accumulated goods. It was necessary to protect these goods and the stationary people who generated them. This assumes some kind of military force and military force assumes the largest and strongest of the species. Military force also assumes hierarchy. This gives us a pattern of the dynamics on the ground. This is the military basis of the culture of empire. In tribal society there were occasional fights between tribes but the basis of the culture was not militarism, they received what their culture defined as the "necessities of life" in another way. Because imperial culture implodes at the center where the greatest and earliest drawdown of ecological energy has taken place, it must continue to make military conquest, for that reason alone.

In the ecological energy flows, we stopped and began to parasitically mine the energies of the living organism. As the accumulation continued, soils began to be exhausted and the landscape denuded from overgrazing. It was necessary to expand and find new soils and grazing on the periphery. This laid the basis for the further dynamics. The males, arranged hierarchically in a military force conquered new lands and often people, who they enslaved to work those new lands for the benefit of the conquerors.

Unlike the matriarchal phase when we moved and did not carry much, the new phase carried with it the psychological factor of materialism as we accumulated possessions. Placing value on material possessions began to be a central focus of the civilized, militarized patriarchy. As the early large empires began to be organized, looting-taking by force- became a central value of the culture.

The imperial culture features a head man or emperor who is surrounded by a male, military/financial elite, who practice female oppression as a cultural norm. This group is undergirded by the productive masses who funnel valuables to the top. The productive masses are arranged in a hierarchal command system under and controlled by the military force. In Babylon, Greece and Rome over half of the population of many cities were slaves and in the lesser known empires as well. Words change from slaves, vassals, peasants, to wage workers but the overall configuration of imperial society has not changed. Now, in the U.S., roughly one percent of the population owns some eighty percent of the wealth of the country and in the rest of the world (except in still existing forager/hunter areas) similar conditions exist.

The imperial culture maintains a parasitic, looting relationship with the earth. This particular human culture is an energy sink; energy is accumulated and exhausted, it does not flow such as with the energies of the ecosystem.

As we have maintained, the culture of empire maintains itself parasitically upon the living earth. In the late industrial version of this culture, industrialism has become the means to power of most countries. One of the principal means to industrial power being sold by the World Bank and other associated institutions, to the less industrialized, is the hydro-electric dam. From this comes the energy to run the factories that will spur further development. The disjunct between the living world and industrialism is shown by the Aswan Dam.

For millennia the annual flooding of the Nile has re-fertilized the fields of the Egyptians. Its biological circulation is so rich that even after the ancient Egyptians destroyed the watershed's incredibly rich natural wetland ecology an empire has been able to exist in this area for thousands of years. The huge Aswan Dam, built in modern times by U.S.S.R. engineers, is finally succeeding in depleting and destroying what remains of Egypt's survival systems. The $1.3 billion dam which halted the flooding of the Nile was planned by the engineers to have two effects; irrigation and hydro-electric generation. Though the dam project is hailed for producing half of the country's electrical "needs" the authors of *Gaia: An Atlas of Planet Management*, report on some of the problems it has created:

"Over one million tons of silt, clay, and sand, which once fertilized downstream fields during periods of flooding, are now silting up Lake Nasser, forcing increased imports of fertilizers. This lock-up of silt also hit downstream industries, starving Cairo brick makers of a vital raw material, while the offshore sardine fisheries, which depended on the flow of nutrients from the Nile, were early casualties. The Nile Delta itself is in retreat.... Simultaneously, problems of soil salinity and water-logging have been accentuated. An FAO (UN Food and Agriculture Organization) study concluded that 35 percent of Egypt's cultivated surface is afflicted by salinity and nearly 90 percent by water-logging. To crown all this, the water-based parasitic disease schistosomiasis has exploded among people living around Lake Nasser."

An investigation revealed that the sandstone bottom of Lake Nasser, the artificial lake created behind the dam, did not seal but allowed considerable seepage through the lake floor. Evaporation from the surface of the 200 mile-long Lake Nasser, and from the extensive system of irrigation ditches is high and there is less total water available for use than before the dam was built.

Worldwide, an estimated 250 million people are infected by schistosomiasis. The parasite which causes the problem, a blood/liver fluke, lives in snails part of its life cycle but lays its eggs in humans. The mature parasite, a fork-tailed worm, affixes itself to humans when the people enter the water of irrigation ditches or the river. The worm bores into the human and seeks out the liver where it lays its eggs. The eggs pass from the person by excretion. As they enter the waterways, they are ingested by the snails in the form of larvae. The parasites drain their human hosts' physical energy. Persons infected in these agricultural countries are able to work only a few hours each day.

The alternate flooding and drying of the land near the Nile formerly controlled snail populations who host part of the worms' life cycle. The flooding washed them out to sea. Since the building of the dam, the snails have multiplied. It is estimated that 70 percent of the population of Egypt is now infected with schistosomiasis.

Sharp declines in agricultural production among a population with one of the world's low ranking average annual incomes, already close to starvation levels, forced the Egyptian government to use a part of the electrical power produced by the new dam to operate fertilizer plants. The application of chemical fertilizers has, to some extent, temporarily offset the losses, but yield is still 20 percent less than in pre-Aswan days.

A result of the new industrial agricultural techniques has been to inject herbicides, insecticides and chemical fertilizers into the now nutrient-poor Nile, through irrigation runoff. This effluent plus the lack of nutrient flow once provided by the river has damaged the five shallow lakes in the Nile Delta. One of these lakes alone formerly yielded 15,000 tons of fish annually for this protein starved nation. The lakes themselves were created when sediments carried by the flooding river created sandbars in the delta, which in turn caused the large shallow lakes behind them. Now that the annual deposition is filling up Lake Nasser rather than flowing downstream, the ocean is eroding the sandbars and soon there will be no lakes. Nineteen thousand people live in this area and are dependent upon the fishing industry in those lakes.

For many years, a sizeable fishing industry had existed off the Mediterranean coast of Egypt. Nearly half of the 18,000 ton annual catch consisted of sardines. When the nutrients of the Nile ceased to be injected into the marine ecology, the Egyptian fish exportation dropped by one-half and the sardine catch went down 500 tons.

Now the waters of the Nile are either evaporating from Lake Nasser or seeping into its sandstone floor, the Mediterranean is deprived of an important fresh water supply. Because of this, the salinity of the entire Mediterranean is rising and threatening all fishing industries of the area.

FOOD FOR THE HUNGRY OR FOOD FOR PROFIT?

For a million years we had "enough" but suddenly the patriarch demanded more. It was not self-sufficiency that was sought. What was being sought was more than enough to live on the earth in tribal style. What this means is that the earth had become a commodity and was forced to produce surpluses for profit and/or power to supply the lifestyle in imperial culture.

One could produce food and habitation from one's own land but surpluses are needed to sell/trade/barter for the other necessities of the imperial lifestyle. This means mining the earth for metals, mining the forests, fish stocks, and soils for surpluses. Surpluses are most easily generated by a specialized mass production system.

This also means coercive power, control, centralization, and uniformity (simplification versus complexity) of which the emperor is the symbol, the center of control. Uniformity exists in the cadres of the military, in mass produced products and with we tractable masses in the empire. Uniformity is a key word in the mass institutions that control our lives. With agriculture the plowman does not live from the fruits of the earth but from his centralized control of the soil and the herder does not hunt the wild herds he controls his own.

TECHNOLOGY ALLOWS THE EARTH'S FERTILITY TO BE EXTORTED MORE EFFICIENTLY

The Roman Empire established Latifundias, huge state-run agricultural centers. After the slave hunters had carried the locals away the Romans brought their system in.

They were able to bring in seeds, root stock, and agricultural techniques and inventions from around the empire. Then they could use the controlled labor to work the land with their big steel bottom plows and their comparatively "advanced" agricultural techniques. These techniques of course were directed toward forcing as much production from the land as possible. This forced up the production from the soil and the growing herds overgrazed and denuded the landscape.

North Africa was once a rich ecosystem. It was the "breadbasket" of both the Greek and Roman empires. Wheat was the big export but many other products were shipped also from the colonies to the "mother country." Now, North Africa is ecologically denuded. The last significant forests were burned in the eleventh century A.D. by the Arab empire when its troops came through headed for Spain which it held until the middle ages. Historians say that Rome moved as much as fifteen million bushels of grain from Egypt and North Africa to the imperial center in some years. Now, some of the Roman port cities of North Africa are ten and fifteen miles from the water. All this has been filled in by erosion material from the exploited countryside.

As the culture of empire spread from the beginning, ecological denudation was progressively visited upon the Indus Valley, the Mid-East, the Mediterranean, the forests and soils of Europe and now the whole world.. In the east, the empire of the Han Chinese devastated the land as they conquered and colonized. Prior to empire, half of China proper was a great temperate forest. Who knows how many amazing species went down with the forest; we will never know. Now little exists in that ecologically destroyed land. Such has been the ecological history of empire and now the entire world is subject to it.

THE NEW CULTURE OF LIVING FROM THE INCREASE

The power to kill- military force; guns, bombs, and police enforce the control possessed by the emperor. The control is also enforced by the cultural conditioning inculcated into our minds and bodies. Our role is to be a productive cog in the emperor's machine. Our role in that movie is not to have power. Power is centralized in the person of the emperor and his military/financial associates.

Our new culture of militant gardeners is vastly more powerful than the emperor's power to kill and destroy. It is decentralization. If each person and small community become self-sufficient they gain power, power to provide for themselves without dependency. Can we imagine a world in which each human by their own efforts can take care of their survival needs? Food, shelter, and clean drinking water are survival items. When one gains the power to feed themselves and house themselves and to create their own human culture by cooperating and encouraging the growth of life, one has achieved real power.

Self-sufficiency means that one does not have to extort ecological fertility from the earth in order to trade with the empire for baubles. Researchers say that there are between five and seven thousand plants in the world that are human edible. There are basically ten plant species in world commerce today.

The reason for this is cultural, (conditioned acceptance of particular foods), and the mechanical efficiency of extracting protein from the soil. For example, one could harvest more protein from an acre of cattails than from an acre of potatoes. (The shoots, tubers and the cattail itself are edible portions). But, mechanical, mass production farming, over large reaches of land cannot be easily introduced for cattails. We still have the element of surplus profits from the soil. Mass production, industrial agriculture can only function with large tracts of land. The large surpluses can finance the machinery and it must be by growing species that can be easily harvested with machines.

The key distinction is that we are growing food to feed hungry people and the mass production system is growing food to make a profit. We are growing a healthy ecosystem and eating (and benefitting in other ways) from the increase. The industrial system is exhausting soils into lifelessness and then using military/economic power to get new "unspoiled" soils to continue the trajectory.

We must have this firmly understood. Our path is not that of fame and fortune in the empire. As we shall see, we will not have massive surpluses of one species grown with row crop agriculture to sell on the market. But, we will have food abundance from a wide diversity of species that occur on our watershed.

PERMANENT AGRICULTURE

Permaculture which we will explore, is not the first ecologically integrated food growing strategy. Our ancient ancestors have practiced such methods especially in rainforest environments for geological periods of time.

A small volume produced by *Cultural Survival* magazine entitled *Indigenous Peoples and Tropical Rainforests*, by Jason W. Clay, summarizes the so far, limited observations that have been made of true rainforest food growing, called swidden. First, the matter of soils is known precisely by most indigenous people. Soil quality is judged by the type of vegetation growing on it. It is judged by its color, taste, smell and by examining its subsoil moisture during various seasons. This means, not that any one spot will be chosen for a plot but that each area is appropriate for plots according to the plants that will subsist best in that environment. The food growing regime will not necessarily involve one or several plots, but may encompass many smaller ones according to the needs.

During clearing of the plots, some of the plant species may be saved. Some of the tree species may be saved also for shade, wind breaks, to attract wild animals that will be used for food or for later use. In the planting one does not simply sow seeds but may use seeds, seedlings, cuttings, tubers and roots. The rainforest gardener may place fifty to one hundred different species in a plot. In arranging the plantings, shade, light, soil, soil moisture, companion plants, nearby trees and other considerations will indicate the creation of micro-climates within the plot. All of these combinations will be transformed according to the different ecological zones that each plot has been located in. As the plot is "feathered" into the mature forest, the matter of local animals is keenly considered in terms of attracting them to the area by having plants in the locale that the animals like and utilize. Anthropologists have discovered that many plots remain in some kind of use for many years. With use, the soil and the growth of different plants in the plot changes. As the years go on, different plants are emphasized, often tending more and more toward bush and tree crops following the cycles of ecological succession. There is mention in the literature of use of plots for 20, 30, and more years. Even after the plot is abandoned people continue to extract food because some plants will reseed themselves or are perennials and the tree crops of course last until the forest cycles back to climax.

One very important observation made by a few of the anthropologists is that this transformation from cleared plot to mature forest follows to a great extent the phases of ecological succession of the natural forest - except the tribal people substitute useful relatives or plants of similar life habits for the plant that would ordinarily be in place during ecological succession. In many cases an outsider may look at a swidden plot and actually not realize that it is not part of the surrounding forest.

The Kayapo´ of the Amazon collect forest plants and replant them near camp and near main trails. The indigenous farmers use at least 54 species of plants to include in these forest fields which are planted in the main camp area and on main trails. Anthropologist D.A. Posey says that a Kayapo´ village may have 500 kilometers of trails that are planted and managed, so that travel may go on for months at a time without resort to the swidden plot produce.

Human cultures around the earth have developed diverse and perpetual ways to feed themselves. In previous times most of the people in societies were involved in food provisioning in some manner. In the past, human cultures have created amazingly diverse and intricate adaptations to the ecological energy flows of the earth. Recently, food provisioning has become industrialized. As industrial mass production is applied to the land, the people are swept off. The ideal situation for an expanding industrialist is that large dams are established with loans from the center of wealth. With the dams, electrical energy can be generated which spurs the industrialization of the society. This is controlled by the industrialist class who provide the machinery and capital. As this proceeds, agriculture is industrialized in the rural areas. The large tracts of land needed are provided by many strategies. One strategy is to flood the country with cheap food produced by highly subsidized crops from the industrialized countries. This bankrupts the small farmers. Another familiar strategy is to simply have the military or clandestinely supported death squads kill the peasants and sweep them away. As the countryside is cleared the impoverished people end up in the cities where they become a cheap labor force for the newly developing industrial system, energized by the electricity provided by the large dams.

MODERN PERMACULTURE

Permaculture (*perma*nent agri*culture*) was established by David Holmgren and Bill Mollison in Australia. These two, who were young men at the time, began to describe a system of food provisioning that rested upon a permanent design of basically, perennial-long lived- plants (trees, bushes, shrubs, forbs, tubers and mushrooms) appropriately spread across the landscape. Since their beginnings they have generated a large body of literature. What they began has now spread world-wide. There are permaculture demonstration centers in many countries along with thousands of people who have been trained in Permaculture design.

A friend told of driving across a huge semi-arid area in Zimbabwe. In the far distance was a spot of green which they drove toward. When they arrived they discovered a thriving Permaculture center covering many acres. The only use of the land for many miles around was by traditional herders, driving the land into desertification. There is little profit in saving the living things of the earth, so Permaculture has been passed hand to hand so to speak, across the globe.

Mollison, in his opus, *Permaculture: A Designers Manual*, states an opening principle - "the only ethical decision is to take responsibility for our own existence and that of our children." The second general principle he states concerns shared energy flows. He says, "cooperation not competition, is the very basis of existing life systems and of future survival."

CREATING A PERMACULTURE DESIGN

THE WATER

The ideal in our restoration ecology is to help the earth heal. We want to encourage the ecosystem to return to its climax state. Some wild areas on our watershed we will leave to their own progression toward climax if they are not already at climax. Other areas that have been subject to human disturbance we would call injured. These injured areas, which would often be most of the watershed, we will restore, but this restoration will be actually scar tissue. By our efforts we will be creating a new ecology that mimics the original. We will include many species from the original but we will also create a much wider diversity of plants, especially those that have human use such as food, oils, gums, resin, construction materials, shade, windbreaks, and many other creative uses.

Say we have already placed ourselves in our ideal situation at the top of a watershed in low hills. We look at the water and where it runs. Water runs both above and below ground. If one is a water dowser or knows one, the underground streams can be determined. We want to have a good understanding of where the surface runoff goes and also how the water moves underground. Our effort will be to retard the water runoff.

Permaculturists say that observation, over time, is the main ingredient in a permaculture design. The planetary ecology has gotten along fine without the humans but humans do have some attributes that can further help out. Humans can observe and humans are mobile. They can help here and there with the water flows, they can seed areas that may be appropriate, they can bring in plants that will increase the diversity; humans can be a valuable asset to a watershed.

Water and soil are items that humans can help with. Soil and water are the basis of the watershed

Strategically placed small dams are an obvious step. These help the water infiltrate the subsoil and also can be the basis of micro-ecologies around the pond. Swales created on sloping ground are simply shallow pits that measure from a few feet to maybe a dozen feet. These are placed on sloping contours. Often a tree is placed in the swale and the extra moisture can support other associated vines and plants in combination. The absorbency of our watershed on the broadscale, will depend largely on the surface soil conditions. As the loose friable soil builds up and the number of plants increases, the infiltration of water increases as it is slowed down and absorbed. We want to recharge the underground aquifers and also retain as much moisture in the soil as possible. As the underground water increases, springs in the area grow stronger and seeps may begin in some areas. In this case water is life.

Beavers can be an essential element in the matter of water infiltration. If we help establish a colony of beavers near the top of the watershed, they will build dams and work downward after they have the upper flow controlled. The beaver pond is a whole micro-ecology. The pond holds silt that runs down helping energize the area. It raises the underground water table around the dam which enables more plant roots to reach water. It creates an environment that allows a whole range of species to exist in a place where formerly there was simply a narrow riparian habitat. In establishing the beavers we first need to plant food for them. When we get a good stand of willows, poplars and other beaver food streamside, then we can bring them in. This is not as difficult as it seems because one simply cuts off branches of willow or poplar and stick them in moist ground and they will root.

When the beaver pond finally silts up or the beavers decide to move for other reasons, the area becomes a lush "beaver meadow," essentially a shelf of highly fertile soil that came to rest behind the beaver dam.

Beavers, a key species in the ecology, have been stripped from much of the U.S. for the fur trade, causing immense harm to the ecology. They continue to be persecuted by agriculturalists who accuse them of damming up irrigation systems and generally being in the way.

Using swales, micro-dams, beavers and increasing the health of the topsoil we will begin to build our capacity for water infiltration and storage. The important water storage is underground where huge amounts can be held to slowly exit in springs and seeps at lower elevations in a slow reliable pace which then increases the fertility base and insures against dry periods.

THE SOIL

The terrestrial realm of life is generally focused in the soil as the primary energy bank or reservoir. Other than marine coral environments, soil is probably the most important organic community on earth. The soil is a very complex community with millions of microscopic organisms in a spoonful. The soil community is comprised of such things as fungi, bacteria, yeasts, algae, protozoans, earthworms, nematodes, arthropods and mollusc fauna. The soil community receives its food from the decomposition of organic material falling on it. Leaves, branches, dead grass, windblown detritus, and dead coyotes all serve to feed the soil. The organisms in the soil function as an energy flow ecology with most organisms serving one or more benefits to its neighbor species including donating its corpse to others down the food chain. Both the decomposition of organic material (eating in the food chain) and the services that species perform for each other are aspects of the ecological energy flow system. This flowing energy system begins in its outer framework with solar energy, wind, and rain and flows through all systems down to the microscopic.

An interesting example of this is the Peruvian anchovy event which deals with geographical energy flows. Toward the end of the 1960's the world financial institutions began to lend money to Peru to purchase new fishing vessels from Scandinavia to catch the abundant stock of anchovies off the coast. The Humboldt Current which sweeps up past Japan to Alaska and then down the continent to Peru, picks up organic sediment from the river mouths along the coast. The organic erosion material carried by the river represents biological energy that charges the ocean ecosystems around the river mouths. This current carries some of that material in deep water until it has an upwelling off the coast of Peru. There it feeds the micro organisms, then up the food chain to a shrimp-like species and then to massive schools of anchovies. These are eaten by sea birds and other predators and their excrement - guano, is deposited on islands off the coast.

In the old days the Incas would mine the guano and take it in backpacks out on their complex road system to be deposited in their food producing areas. The energy pathway would then find its way to the humans. From solar warming, to ocean currents, to rivers running with silt, to ocean food chains the energy pathway continued toward the Inca terrace gardens.

In the modern system the catch of anchovies was spectacular after the Peruvians began using modern fishing vessels. In the final year before the collapse of the anchovy stock this catch represented over one fifth of the annual ocean fish catch. Its energy pathway bypassed the seabirds, and the anchovies were squeezed for fish oil and ground up for fish meal which was sent past the hungry Peruvians, to the industrialized countries, to be inserted into the agricultural system as fertilizer and animal food. The energy pathway was finally ended as ham and eggs on the breakfast table. Inasmuch as the industrial system does not use composting toilets, the pathway ended there in an energy sink called a wastewater treatment plant. (The energy loop is not completed to the soil fertility.)

The industrial system did not stop with the anchovy, it also mines the guano (phosphate) and injects this into the industrial agricultural system. Phosphate, an essential ingredient in artificial fertilizer, is mined from islands and seacoasts world-wide. This lynch-pin resource is, at this period of history, almost gone and the small governments of those islands are searching for other sources of income. Searching also is the world food system but no replacement for this essential material has been found. Meanwhile the food system hangs in the balance.

The Peruvian anchovy stock has not recovered. Often when this occurs other species rush to fill the food chain niche that the impacted species occupied and the species has real trouble regaining it population. The Peruvian anchovy joined the dozens of ocean species around the planet that have had this experience. Many people remember John Steinbeck's books that included scenes from the fishing docks and processing plants in Monterey, California. That stock of anchovy is long gone from the waters off shore but some of the docks and buildings remain for tourist to see what had been Steinbeck's world.

Another interesting example that illustrates not the food chain but the non-food chain energy flow system, is from the old growth forests of the U.S. Pacific Northwest. In this forest an important contribution is made by the actual body of various mushroom species which are the mycelium which are small strands that spread in vast acreage under the forest floor. There the mycelium merge with the root tips of above-ground plants, particularly the Douglas Fir, and exchange nutrients. The mushroom is the fruiting sexual body that pops up above the ground. When the mushroom pops up it is nibbled by the local mice. They then excrete these spores, planting them around the forest, thus helping the whole.

When clearcuts exist in the forest this hampers the whole system. This happens because the mice are reluctant to leave the canopied forest and enter the clear cut and spread the fungi because the mice are subject to the flying raptors overhead. Thus, the forest is denied that flow of assistance from abundant mycelium. This is an example of factors in the ecological energy flow system that are apart from the simple energy flow of the food chain, of one organism eating another. These non-food chain energy flows are subtle and complex and we humans still have much to learn about them.

With all of the eating along the food chain in the soil community, nutrient substances are produced which are taken up by the photosynthesizing plants above ground. Plants do not eat dirt. They absorb nutrients in solution in the soil. The plants and the soil create a circulating energy system in which the plant grows up out of the soil which feeds it. It combines with solar energy to increase biomass and then the organic debris from this growth falls back to feed the soil. From this circulation a "profit" happens that allows for a buildup both of the fertility of the soil and also its gross amount. This "savings bank" of the earth, the accumulation of topsoil, is very laborious. Researchers estimate that it requires three hundred to one thousand years to accumulate each inch of topsoil in prime soil building ecosystems such as old growth forests, mature prairies and primary wetlands. Soil buildup is slower in other ecosystems.

When we find soils that are six inches deep or a foot deep we can see how long it took the living system to build up this energy. If we live in a civilized environment we can look around us and see how many years of biological life is removed to level a plot for a house or shopping mall.

The matter of the soil on our watershed is of extreme importance and it must be guarded from erosion, exhaustion or other harm. The present environmental crisis began when the first agrarian villages were put up. By six thousand years ago Babylon was in full swing. Today, one-third of the arable land of Iraq cannot be used because of the salinization of the soil from Sumerian/Babylonian irrigation. At one time the Tigris and the Euphrates rivers each emptied independently into the Gulf. Now they join and empty into the Gulf far downstream because the massive load of erosion material, caused by overgrazing and agriculture, has filled in the Gulf for one hundred and eighty-five miles. This has created the wetlands where the "marsh arabs" now live! This and six thousand years of imperial history are our inheritance.

THE TREES

Trees are a fundamental and irreplaceable species on the earth. Trees give wood for construction, they give fire for food and other uses, they give food, shade, erosion control, wind breaks, create the environment for soil generation, they moderate temperatures, and there are many other benefits. Trees relationship to water is an essential ingredient in their guilds. Guilds are cooperating groups of species centered around a main species. These can be insects, animals, plants, mushrooms, and so forth. Usually, the tree is a central species. The various species in the tree's guild benefit from its water gathering and evapotranspiration which moistens the area. Trees also produce water by a process called "fog drip." When fogs come through a forest the moisture collects of the leaf surfaces and some falls to the forest floor to enter the ground water. Also as the cool night air touches the tree leaf a condensate appears (dew) that drips to the forest floor. Up to 35 percent of moisture under trees can be produced by "fog drip," over time, depending on the climate and tree species.

Half of the rain falling on forests is transpired back to the atmosphere. This creates rain as the microscopic droplets become seed forms for the precipitation of atmospheric moisture. This creates rain that falls further downwind.

PLACING THE TREE

The placing of trees on our watershed is a central element in our design. Long periods of observation should be involved. We have to think about the wind flow, the water flow, the soil nature, what other guild species that we might add that will adapt to that micro-climate, human needs, and many other things. A group of trees will raise the water table and moderate temperature-humidity in that area. Around the house, for example, we would use deciduous trees that lose their leaves annually, in certain areas to shade the area during summer and during winter after the leaves fall, sunlight would be allowed through.

It is a principle of Permaculture that each species must serve at least two purposes in the design. When we plant guilds we have a number of species that live together and through various routes, help each other with nutrient, moisture, shade, wind protection, insect attraction or diversion and many other things. This we must constantly keep in mind.

When we look at a mature forest we see a stand of trees that are often of the same species or a few species and sometimes a mixed forest, but in a tropical rainforest with its great diversity there are often more species of trees on one acre than the total number of tree species on the North American continent. Thus, we have choices depending upon where we live.

We, of course, are not immediately creating an old growth forest. We are creating scar tissue and we are also creating a way to live on the earth that can serve all of the species, including us.

We will be planting food forests. The authors Douglas and Hart give us some valuable comparisons in their seminal work, *Forest Farming*. They say that a herder can produce an average of 200 pounds of meat from an acre of rich pasture. In comparison, we see that the same space could produce one-half ton of cereal grain, seven tons of apples, or 15-20 tons of flour from the pods of honey locust trees (which is superior in nutritional value to cereal grains).

Some average yields of tree crops help illuminate these tremendous differences (and these are in addition to other benefits such as gums, oils, wood, etc.). Production from an acre of African locust beans-10-15 tons, carob-

18-20 tons, mulberries- 8-10 tons, persimmons- 5-7 tons, chestnuts- 7-11 tons, and dates- 4-7 tons.

The above figures are for plantings with normal orchard spacing. We will be placing trees much more sparsely but there will be interplantings with tall bushes, low bushes, forbs, vines and tuber producing plants along with mushroom plantings. This will greatly increase the food production on a per acre basis. This is why we say that we can grow more food per acre than the industrial system, while maintaining the soil (because its not tilled and it is fed by the above ground plants' organic material falling on it), and restoring the ecosystem (our Permaculture is building scar tissue and edging the ecosystem back to its health of climax biodiversity). It should be emphasized also that we are basing our design on perennial plants for the most part. We would of course use some annuals and biennials (one year and two year life cycles). We would choose these short lived plants so that they are species that self-seed, which will add to the permanency of our design.

THE ASSOCIATES OF TREES

Permaculture as a cultural institution has adopted a simple, basic guide; a design which views one's place in a series of concentric circles. David Holmgren cautions that this should not be turned into a blueprint but simply a general guide. These concentric circles divide one's place into four or five "zones." At zone zero is the homestead. In zone one is a fully integrated garden. This is the kitchen garden. Ideally a person could walk out of the kitchen door and pick herbal seasonings, an onion or other food that may be needed for the meal being cooked. In zone two, further from the house is the place for irrigated orchards and small livestock. Zone three in this idealized plan is unirrigated and is devoted to commercial specialty crops, pasture, plantations, dams and large livestock. Zone four represents managed rangeland, forests and wetlands. Outside of zone four we hope is the wilderness area where little management takes place and life develops by its own design.

When we put this rough guide on the ground we observe the land that we have. Each place is different so we will adjust appropriately. We need to understand the rainfall patterns, the water flow contours on the ground and which soils are absorbing water well and which are not. We would study the wind patterns during each season. Which direction the prevailing winds come from and when is important. The slope of the land is also important, as well as which aspects are facing the sun in which seasons.

We are creating scar tissue, and any indigenous plants remaining, we would first look at in terms of keeping them on the land, and they will help give us clues to soil fertility and soil moisture where they are standing. We will know the different species habits. This is, whether the plant likes poor soil or rich, acid or alkaline and whether the plant likes very wet areas or dry. Where indigenous plants are located will also give us clues on similar plants that exist in our inventory of cultivars (human selected plants). For example one might have wild grapes in a certain area. This would be a place to investigate the possibility of placing domesticated varieties of grapes.

One of our purposes here is to increase species diversity. We are looking for niches in which to place a plant where none have been before. When we have the trees placed then will come the high bushes. Most of these useful bushes will be fruit such as elderberries, sea buckthorn, smaller plum trees, paw paws, medlars, or pomegranate. Smaller bushes could be blueberries, gooseberries, raspberries and those sorts of plants. We would include vining plants such as kiwi, grape, chayote, and climbing or vining bean plants such as the scarlet aztec climber which with care can go perennial. (Some garden plants in northern latitudes are actually perennials but they freeze each winter. If they can be protected from the freeze they will become perennial).

We then look for more garden type plants that are preferably perennial or plants that easily reseed themselves. Some examples of well known plants of this type are horseradish, asparagus, rhubarb, jerusalem artichokes, globe artichokes and potatoes that can take care of themselves such as the purple peruvian variety.

Tuber plants such as taro, sweet potatoes and yams are another opportunity to "stack" our design. Mushrooms also must be considered. Because of our progressing cultural institutions, we can be very specific in which variety of mushrooms we plant where and for what purpose. The one outstanding institution from which spores can be obtained is the commercial mushroom center named *Fungi Perfecti*.

As our design progresses we are alert for opportunities to plant species that feed our friends. We need bee flowers, butterfly flowers, beaver trees, and plants that appeal to wild turkeys, deer, rabbits or whatever animals occur on our watershed. Some of these animals will be providing several benefits to the whole, for example, the bees will be both helping pollinate and creating honey. Other animals that are attracted may be eaten on occasion.

We will have the entire inventory of domesticated animals available to us. Many of these have more than one purpose. For example, ducks do weeding in some areas, chickens can also be useful in consuming garden trimmings, their manure is very useful and they can be put in certain areas to control insects.

If the climate and bioregion is right for us we can also commence aquaculture. Especially in our wastewater/ sewerage treatment ponds that will have potable water running from the last pond, we will have the opportunity to create a full aquaculture program. This will include aquatic plant species specific to each pond down the line, stream-side plants and the array of fishes, frogs, ducks and any other species that will fit.

David Holmgren suggests a set of nine principles to use when creating a permaculture design over time. These principles are: observe and interact; catch and store energy; obtain a yield; apply self-regulation and accept feedback; use and value renewable resources and services; produce no waste (everything cycles); design from patterns to details; integrate rather than segregate; use small and slow solutions; use and value diversity; use edges and value the marginal; and creatively use and respond to change.

THE NEW COOKBOOK

Euro-American cookbooks are a prescription for destroying the world. Each culture's means of producing food from the earth is a reflection of how that society is organized. No one controls the food of the forager-hunters. Using their culturally taught knowledge, each of them can go out and find their own food. This is reflected in their loosely organized society of free individuals where no one controls the food supply and no one owns the earth. In a rice eating society, there is the administration of the irrigation systems that water the rice. This requires centralized control so that each area gets water when those rice paddies need it. This assumes some kind of hierarchal and centralized control within the social organization. It also means that the ecology of the area is wiped out to clear the land for those rice paddies.

In the case of the Indo-Europeans a specialized relationship to the land has developed. All of Europe speak Indo-European languages except the Basque of Spain. The Indo-Europeans were part of that group who in ancient times originated in the area of Eastern Turkey and present day Armenia. The Indo-Aryans were the branch that invaded India, the Indo-Iranians invaded Persia and the Indo-Europeans invaded Europe.

As wheat and barley were wild plants in the mid-east which they domesticated, they brought these along. In northern Europe they found kale growing wild. From kale they developed cabbage, kohlrabi, brussels sprouts, collards, and others, all in the *brassica* family. They also added domesticated livestock, especially the cow and they later added pigs, goats and fowl. It is this system of agriculture and the cook books which give instruction of how to prepare these grains and animals that is eliminating the ecology and ruining the soils of much of the world. Now the Euro-American cook book is nearly obsolete as we live in an industrially organized and centralized society, our food is industrially produced and industrially processed so that to a large degree the food is prepared in a central location and shipped out to us. This centralized configuration is reflected in the social organization where only a few giant corporations control much of the industrial food supply and an even smaller number of people control the giant corporations.

Our new culture will need to write a new cook book. We are growing a wide diversity of foods. Many of these plants are exotic and new to our palate. Rather than eat all year around of the ten basic industrial food plants, we will be harvesting all year from our wide variety of foods as they come to harvest. This will require creativity in cooking and adaptation as we learn to adjust to this widened variety of foods.

THE POSTAGE STAMP GARDEN THAT WILL KEEP YOU ALIVE FOREVER

We are discussing the creation of the new world, but this also means survival. In this vein we must mention another cultural creation that can be a fall back position or a food production area that can anchor one's homestead until the permaculture design is up and growing and providing adequate food.

Outside of the small Northern California town of Willits, is the Ecology Action Center. On a small piece of land on a dry hillside covered with sparse oak trees, John Jeavons, Carol Cox and others have solved the world food problem. Groups come from all over the planet to learn their biointensive gardening method. They come to learn how to grow a garden on 1,000 square feet that will feed one person forever, while also growing sufficient compost to replenish the soil fertility - on that same space.

This is it. This is an answer to the world food problem. The fact that this exists and is known about by world leaders helps us sharpen our social, political and economic analytical skills as to why this has not been already implemented across the world.

The System taught by Jeavons relies on raised beds, composting, rich soil, close planting and importantly only particular varieties of specific species are used. The variety of each species used is laboratory tested for nutritional content so that a full and adequate diet is produced from the combination. Ecology Action also has a small seed company called Bountiful Gardens from which high quality seed may be obtained.

WE HAVE CREATED AN IMPORTANT CULTURAL INSTITUTION

Following the genius of Bill Mollison and David Holmgren, thousands of people around the planet have now contributed to the continuing creation of Permaculture as a social institution that is benefitting us as we proceed toward the new world. What has been given above is only a brief sketch of the whole. Coming from all continents and bioregions, the ideas, new species, new techniques, new discoveries manifest constantly in the literature of Permaculture.

Bill Mollison in particular has produced a large body of written work as well as articles and videos. There exist a number of Permaculture periodicals on several continents that bring out writings and hands-on ideas. Permaculture organizations and societies exist on all continents. The number of trained Permaculture Design teachers now number in the thousands.

CHAPTER THREE

SHELTER

I once walked through an ancient pueblo ruin in New Mexico with a Native American who had grown up in a Native American pueblo. A person in the party asked him why the rooms were so small in the pueblo building. He replied that his ancestors didn't live in rooms but lived on the earth and only used the rooms for inclement weather or other purposes. This describes a life style and a cultural way of relating to the earth. We have already created an image in our Permaculture design of the surroundings of our shelter. Now we can look at alternative shelter construction. Some of these methods being used are very ancient and some are newly created. All of them are hand made by people like you and me.

Alternative house creation is a very personal act. Those who will live in the house will design the house and participate in the building of it. The house will become a part of the landscape and part of the design surrounding it. In earlier days, even in industrial culture, people spoke of the, "old home place." Often this was a farm or ranch but it also could have been a home where the grandparents lived or where the family had lived for generations. This personal sense of having roots has been lost with the rush of mechanical, technological society. When one moves from apartment to apartment or when one upscales from one suburb to the next higher in luxury, one simply moves from box to box. It is not like being there in the home place.

When one works with the land, with the soil, and with the living things, encouraging them to grow, one develops a sense of place, a sense of being at home on the earth. This is very important, this feeling of being a legitimate being on the face of the earth. Each person has a birthright of being on the earth and having a home place that offers sustenance and shelter.

We who have suffered the dysfunction of being living human organisms in a dead mechanical world need this contact. We must restore this ongoing condition of existence. This is our two million year inheritance. This is also an important aspect of our new cultural creation. We are suggesting the creation of a new kind of human culture where the person, family, and tribe lives in one place for many generations. To our alienated, shifting perspective this seems strange, even threatening. Nonetheless we will travel, visit other places, but we will have "the old home place."

LOCATING THE STRUCTURE

Before we set the cornerstone of our handmade house we need to select a location. Where one "makes camp" is of vital importance. It is best if one simply has a "feeling" for it. Observation, meditation, and contemplation are all called for. Also suggested is a study of the earth energies that are flowing in the area as well as great focus on the water drainage away from the building(s).

Ancient traditions held and modern dowsers report, that there are force lines of fine energies that travel over the surface of the earth. These are called Dragon Lines and Tiger lines in China. In the West they could be called simply earth energy lines or Ley Lines. There are negative lines and positive lines. Dowsers find that important ancient edifices are usually involved with energy lines and also with what dowsers call blind springs or water domes, under the ground that do not come to the surface and flow. Chartes Cathedral for example has positive energy lines running outside and around it as well as inside in crucial areas. In addition there is a water dome located under the main alter. It is the belief of people that investigate such things that these energies have impact on human consciousness and human health.

Some call them power spots or sacred sites. Some people feel that these energies are the Chi, Orgone or Etheric energy of the earth, analogous to the energy lines that acupuncturists deal with in the human body. These lines can be manipulated by dowsers. They can be obstructed, channeled or diverted according the needs of the siting of one's shelter.

Another important consideration is the observation of wind patterns and prevailing winds. Unlike a row of houses in a suburb, we will have the luxury of building in natural locations. There might be canyons, ridges, large stands of trees or other impediments channeling winds near a proposed site. The prevailing winds from southeast to northeast in the northern hemisphere are a constant and should be allowed for.

Even the present industrially produced house could lower the energy bill, with no added construction cost, by siting it at a proper angle with the sun and putting certain windows in solar locations. The fact that this is not normally done shows what a dinosaur that industry is. With the alternative, hand made house this is different. We would make full solar assessment of our site. Depending on the climate we might want to site the building on a south facing slope or north facing slope or other feature of the landscape.

This essay will only consider passive solar construction. A normal person looking at the information already given about our planetary situation would not opt for active solar design that needs artificial energy to move the heat and cool around. It is easy to fall into the trap of trying to "save the world." That is, people who are heavily conditioned by civilized culture try to find the silver bullet that will save it. They try to find more energy, more efficient food production, population control and so forth so that conditions can be maintained just as they are. The information presented here, contrarily, indicates that there will be a mass die-off. We are preparing the new culture that will flourish after that.

The good news is, just like the 1,000 square foot garden that will feed one person forever, we have examples of solar houses that function with no artificial energy. This is very important. Our resources are abundant. We have a food growing plan (Permaculture) that can produce more food per acre than the industrial system and we have operational examples of solar houses that can function comfortably with no external energy input to drive heating and cooling.

WATER

Developing water sources takes great care. Whether we have springs, cisterns, wells, creeks, rivers or a combination of these we need to take care that the water balance is maintained. That is, we don't want to drain the water table with a well, nor do we want to destroy any ecology of a stream or river by excess diversion. A basic question that we can ask is, "Where does the water and food come from and where does it go?" Our food is now coming from our Permaculture design on the watershed and our water source needs to be developed. Cisterns are used in many places around the world. Usually these hold water gathered from roofs.

The Nabatean culture that inhabited the Negev Desert from 200 B.C. to about 100 A.D. when they were wiped out by the Roman and then Byzantine empires, used ingenious methods of water storage. These people were expert rock carvers. Some may recognize them by the "Rose City of Petra," their capital, whose buildings were carved out of canyon rock in the Negev. These people carved cisterns out of rock. Scholars state that the entire society held several million of gallons of water in storage in these rock cisterns. They also used plaster, which is created by smelting limestone with a hot fire. They would dig a large hole in the ground at the bottom of a drainage and plaster the walls of the excavation. Some of these cisterns of the Nabateans are said to be still in use by Bedouins in the area.

Our challenge is similar. We need to develop many creative ways to store water if we are anywhere but a very wet environment. One typical restoration technique that has been used successfully is the building of small check dams around an area.

This simple expedient allows enough extra water to infiltrate to raise water tables which we then might easily reach with a hand dug well. This could be pumped by windmills or hand pumps.

Auroville, India, an intentional eco-village and member of the Global Ecovillage Network, has created a large array of check dams on their property as well as leading the project for poor farmers in thirty-two villages in the surrounding area. In their area of India there is a two month per year rainfall period so it becomes important to increase water storage in any way possible. In planting well over a million trees and creating many check dams, they have raised the water table of the area significantly. This is a basic step in restoring the ecology of this denuded region.

Another part of this equation is that in the present industrial society, drinking water is used for all purposes. What we need is simply drinking and cooking water. With a compost toilet, water usage is reduced. Grey water, that is, non-sewerage water from sinks and kitchen, can be reused for garden irrigation or for tree crops.

Some of our water would experience an energy transformation by traveling through solar panels before it enters the kitchen as hot water. A flat plate solar collector with pipes running inside of it can heat water up to 180 degrees. This water is thermosiphoned. When the solar panel is below the storage tank, usually a commercial hot water tank, the hot water rises into the tank. The bottom of the tank is often connected by a pipe to the bottom of the solar collector. This allows the colder water to cycle upward as the water heats.

With our compost toilet, grey water irrigation and composting of kitchen wastes, we have completed the circle. This allows us to meet the principle of no waste, so that waste becomes material for another beneficial energy transformation.

CREATING SHELTER FROM LOCAL MATERIALS

Local materials such as logs, sawn wood, stone, strawbale and earth can be used for shelter creation. Earth can be used in a number of ways. Walls made of adobe are characteristic of the earlier era of the Southwestern U.S.. Adobes are mud bricks made from mud and straw. Not just any earth is used. Many traditional families in the Southwest have their favorite (and often secret) locations for obtaining just the right kind of earth with the mixture of clay, topsoil and small gravel that they like to use.

Cob is another use of earth. In building a cob wall one forms balls of wet earth mixture and places it on the top of the wall as it is built up. A section is built up and left to dry. The builder then returns and adds another layer until the desired height is achieved.

Rammed earth is a very simple material. It requires forms much like the form into which cement is poured to create foundations or walls. Earth is simply dug at the site and rammed into the form. As the wall reaches height, the form is simply moved along until it comes to the planned end of the wall.

Another technique associated with earth material has been developed by Nader Khalili, a Persian architect. He was concerned about houses in his homeland that experience frequent earthquakes. During the earthquakes, roofs often fall-in, injuring or killing the residents. Khalili developed a vaulted ceiling made with the same adobe bricks as the walls. He then fired the entire house by closing it up and igniting barrels of kerosene inside. This "cured" and solidified the house much like a pottery vase. Using this process, the walls may be also covered with clays which create a porcelain interior with any design and colors one wants.

An ancient method called wattle and daub is a useful technique. With this technique one creates a framework of wood, reeds, bamboo or other local materials and then applies mud to the frame. Wattle and daub is often used in Africa and other tropical areas. Saplings, reeds, bamboo and even vines are sometime useful building materials depending on what is being created; walls, fences, or other constructions.

Straw bale is another recently popular wall building material. Rice straw seems to be the material of choice. Usually this is done with post and beam construction. With this method a wooden framework is erected. The beams on a solid, high foundation hold up the header beams across the top of the wall. The bales are then in-filled between the foundation and the header beam at the top of the wall. Load bearing straw bale walls can be also built. The bales are stacked overlapping and rods are inserted down through the bales for stability. A header beam is placed along the top of the walls and the roof installed on it.

All of these materials; log, earth, straw or stone provide very good insulating capacities. These materials also allow a house to "breathe." In recent years, industrially manufactured houses have been produced that are tightly sealed. Inasmuch as many of the materials used in those houses are poisonous, this has created a huge allergenic problem.

THE SOLARIUM

Often a solar greenhouse is constructed on the sun side of the house. These greenhouses when properly insulated and vented can add to the family food supply as well as help heat the house in cool times. The greenhouse has abundant heat sinks that catch the heat and hold it, releasing it during the night. These heat sinks may be specialized walls, called trombe walls. These walls are dark colored on the sun facing side, with vents at the back allowing heat to migrate into a room. Containerized water is often used as a heat sink by filling up large barrels, painting them black and placing them strategically in the solarium. Another addition is a heavy masonry floor which can hold heat after being heated with sunlight.

One maintains an intimate relationship with a hand made alternative house. In addition to maintenance chores there is the everyday managing of the breathing house. There are vents to be opened morning and evening- the air flow must be managed. Insulating curtains may need to be drawn or opened. This is not push button living but we will have plenty of time to do these things in our new culture.

THE SHAPE OF THE SHELTER

We denizens of industrial society are accustomed to a fragmented and disintegrating culture. Living spaces reflect this. We have studio apartments for the single social isolate and then we have the classic family dwelling built for mom, dad, and 2.4 children. In our new culture we will be building structures for use by extended families and even larger affinity groups. Fortunately, when building with local materials and building by hand (in what would become a "barn raising" among friends) we can build as many rooms as we need and to the size that we need.

Living in a hand made house is very different. The house breathes. It is made of natural materials. There are not necessarily any sharp lines. These materials can be shaped and the lines softened so that a very different ambiance is achieved.

THE OTHER REASON WE WANT TO LIVE IN A HAND MADE HOUSE

Industrially manufactured houses are poisonous. Pressure treated wood contains arsenic, fibreboard contains urea formaldehyde, plywood often contains phenol and urea formaldehyde, and particle board gives off formaldehyde. Petrochemical paint, polyurethane foam, plastic carpets, polyvinyl tiles, combustion gases from cooking and heating, household chemicals, and insulation materials often contain and give off noxious and poisonous gases and particles. This aspect, if no other, gives us reason to create our own hand made shelter.

CHAPTER FOUR

HUMAN CULTURE

THE CULTURAL DYNAMICS OF EMPIRE

In order to live on the earth, the human species has to be able to keep the earth alive, because we live from the living earth. In order to keep the earth alive we will have to create a new human culture as the one we have has produced today's reality.

When the inversion occurred from forager/hunter culture to agriculture/empire culture, we stopped moving. We established *civis,* "house." We began to establish villages and fields on the most fertile soils. We began to graze domesticated animals on the landscape. We established a system of control over life and the ecology that had not been done when we were forager/hunters. As forager/hunters we experienced a field of reality inhabited by forms, energies, and events that obviously sprang from a source of great power, a source that could manifest the earth and cosmos and keep it running. In the face of such power we were humble. With the forager/hunters, their culture encouraged the experience of the power behind the forms. In imperial culture the intellect is encouraged and people are conditioned to see that matter is "dead" and biological life is alive but only insignificantly so. With a source of such power and fruitfulness a forager/hunter would not assume to make significant alterations. Is not the flower perfect and does not the cool spring water quench the thirst? Forager/hunters do not live by controlling the earth and the life that lives on it. Like all other organisms we lived by adaptation to the ecological energy flows of the earth.

Anthropologists say that forager/hunters work about five hundred hours per adult person a year, to provide their needs of living on the earth. (Traditional agriculturalists such as the Pueblo/Hopi work an average of one thousand hours per year, live shorter lives, and have more illness. The modern wage worker works two thousand hours a year and appears to be kept alive only by constant medical attention and drugs.) In the case of the !Kung Bushmen who live in one of the most difficult places on earth, the Kalahari Desert of Southern Africa, the proportion of people over 60 years of age is 10 percent. This is slightly below the industrial countries but considerably exceeds the "Third World" countries. The average daily protein intake of this group (93.1 grams) was exceeded by only ten countries of the world.

Anthropologists also say that these people enjoy almost perfect health and are normally happy. The description of the !Kung Bushmen is one of people in a very hostile environment. Forager/hunters who lived in areas of great ecological fecundity such as the diverse forests of the eastern seaboard of the U.S. must have enjoyed a life of great abundance and leisure.

We in civilization have been culturally conditioned by the idea of linear progress. (Ignore for the moment that there is no infinite linear increase or growth system in the cosmos but there are infinite circles and cycles.) Linear increase is a fundamental tenet of our reality view. One of our cherished images is the simple image of the progress of "man the tool maker." In this child's image of human existence on earth, we focus on "tools" as being the gauge of human "progress." In this tale, humans once lived in caves and learned how to make tools. These tools at first were crude but now through progress we have tools to take us to the moon. This, in the conditioned view, places the most important value of the industrial society - tools - in the center. There is no thought of the sublime social institutions that we may have created; there is no mention of human happiness and satisfaction, only the story of the tools. (The story also leaves out mention of any cultures such as the Australian Aborigines who did not use stone tools but only wooden ones which have long since dissolved and are lost to the civilized narrative of history.)

Now, we take this simple image of linear increase and compare it to the hours of work of each lifestyle above and we see that it does not add up. To compound this, we find that anthropology has record of traditional agriculturalist groups who have taken up a forager/hunter lifestyle when available, which offered a superior way of life.

We also have to look at the history of the empires for eight thousand years, right down to the present and see that most of the people living in civilization for thousands of years have not come up to the living conditions of forager/hunters living in one of the most difficult places on the globe!

What this "progress" describes is a progression of tools only, which has nothing to do with the social conditions that people live with. The fact that we in our era live on the verge of planetary suicide, ecological and nuclear, and snidely look askance at primitives who are very crude while we prepare to kill billions with nuclear weapons should give us pause and it also should encourage us to look more precisely at what this word progress really means.

Consider those first agriculturalists. They have crossed a great divide, a great chasm. As forager/hunters they perceived the field of reality as being alive. They perceived it as having great power and providing for them by its fruitfulness. Then, let us propose, they made that great and fateful decision. "We are no longer satisfied with what the cosmos provides; we will use our intellect to force the cosmos to give us more." This changed our spiritual relationship to the earth and cosmos. We have now exerted the impulse of accumulation and we have placed a positive value on that material accumulation. We also changed our relationship with the living earth. When the U.S. was forcing Native Americans onto reservations, some refused to farm saying it was immoral to put a plow into the breast of Mother Earth. With the incipient agriculturalist of old, this sentiment had to be muted and it was. They invented the sky gods. The sky gods sit on a cloud somewhere out in the sky and they are sacred. Down here on earth are just dirt and trees and nothing is sacred; it's all there for our exploitation because it is simply dead matter or plants, trees and bushes that have no value in and of themselves. This is a functional origin of materialism in the culture of civilization and describes the great divide between the respect for life and living things and the respect for accumulations of dead material objects and gold.

We have that original agriculturalist now, there with his house, flocks and fields. A number of consequences flow from that fact. Because he is stationary and is accumulating, he must organized some way for he and the other villagers to protect their material accumulation. This assumes a military, coercive basis of social organization. If there is a military force that protects the new cultural project, then the larger of the species, the males, have to be in charge. Here we have set up a male dominated hierarchal command system.

As the new agriculturalists pursue their course of accumulation they exhaust the soil of their fields and denude the landscape by overgrazing. This forces them to expand to new soils and new undamaged pastures as it is the biological energy of the soils and ecosystem that funds their imperial project.

Historically, over the eight thousand years we see the time-line of empires rise and fall. The empire swells, based on the ecological fertility that it is sucking up. As that fertility dwindles in the center, the empire is finally unable to expand further into new energy sources on its periphery. It then implodes. We see the ruined climax ecologies of China, the Indus River Valley, Iraq, Greece, North Africa, and Europe that are left behind. Now the culture of empire is being globalized and there remains very little climax ecology on the planet. The climax ecology is the standard of health of the earth.

This project endures because of the element of control in the culture. We don't pick the fruit from the trees when it is offered, we control the earth and force it to produce. Thus the culture of empire has run a net deficit of the biological energy since its inception. It lives and grows by exhausting the soils, deforestation, and overgrazing. In our functional image, the patriarch at the top controls everything. This is a slave relationship. He controls the men "under" him, he controls women and children, and he controls his biological slaves which he uses to translate soil and ecosystem fertility into protein. This is the emperor who owns an empire and has a monopoly on violence. He has created a culture of materialism, militarism, hierarchy, patriarchy, and linear growth.

The emperor has alienated himself from the living reality with his sky gods. He has become alienated from the living world which has become a commodity/resource. He has become an individualist sitting on his hoard. He no longer participates in an economy where food and goods are distributed through familial systems of sharing such as forager/hunters. He became alienated, abstracted, when sharing changed to profit and further was abstracted into currency. His voluminous oral literature became abstracted into writing. His spirituality became abstracted into the sky gods. He went on then, for eight thousand years, killing, maiming, enslaving, and destroying the life of our earth.

THE PSYCHOLOGY OF EMPIRE

Fear is the fundamental of this cultural form. The assertion is that the basic spiritual shift in consciousness was from a reality-view that saw the entire cosmos as alive and fecund to a reality-view that saw the earth as meaningless matter to be used to battle the scarcity of the world. On the one hand the human is at home on the earth sharing space with other cooperating neighbor species in a reality of mystery and power. On the other hand one lives in a world of accumulation where fear of scarcity and survival is prevalent. On a more profound level, one has spiritually severed oneself from a reality of participation in a living, abundant world and created a reality of scarcity and violence in which one is a competitive isolate in a meaningless world.

When a tree sprouts in the forest it begins to assemble life. The tree extends its roots and no doubt makes contact with the mycelium of a mushroom, extending its energy flow and living relationship. It raises leaves to the sun and connects with that living energy system. It connects with water in the air and soil, it connects with the diverse soil community. The tree unifies energies in its living systems. The life of the earth functions in its balanced way because each being lives according to its particular nature. The decentralized power of all life resides in each being. The pattern of empire culture in contrast, is to centralize power over life and consequently the natural patterns disintegrate.

A golf course, for example, appears very neat and orderly. With its edged borders, well watered grass and trees, it represents the epitome of orderliness to the mind conditioned by the culture of civilization. In the reality of earth life, created and conditioned by cosmic forces, it is a gross disorder. Where once stood a life potentiating, balanced and perpetual, dynamic, climax ecosystem with its diverse circulating energies and manifold variety of beings, there are now a few varieties of designer plants kept alive by chemicals and artificial water supplies. A staff of maintenance people are kept busy battling the integrated life of the earth that attempts to rescue this wound by sending in the plants, animals and other life forms that are naturally adapted to live in the area.

Human life in the culture of civilization is severed from its source in a similar way. It is alienated from its source. This profoundly effects the psychology of the humans involved. On the one hand we humans as forager/hunters stand on the earth. When we eat from the earth we have a certain dignity and security. Each one of the tribe has the culturally given knowledge of how to walk out on the earth and find food and shelter. It is a direct and intimate relationship. In the culture of empire people are dependent on other people for their food and shelter. They do not get their sustenance from their intimate relationship with the earth but from their manipulation of other humans in some manner. They exist in a vast productive mechanism that sucks materials from the earth to build an artificial reality such as a shopping mall where humans manipulate each other in order to achieve the needs of their existence.

The integrated nature of the organic form of the whole world and the adaptation of each form within is demonstrated by their place in the balanced metabolism of the whole. There is an organism within organic life that does not practice this balance within the metabolism. It practices a linear growth plan. This organism is the cancer cell within biological life and it does accurately reflect an analogy with the culture of civilization. The cancer cell breaks the cooperative and sharing relationship with its fellow cells and becomes "God" as it were. "I am not satisfied with what has been given with this body, I shall create a body of my own design." Instead of remaining integrated and adapted to the body it is part of, the cancer cells create a body of their own design and use the host's body as its energy feed. This unlimited growth system of the cancerous tumor body built by the cells begins to colonized the body, establishing new cancer tumor bodies, all functioning in a parasitic metabolism until the host body dies.

THE FEARFUL SEPARATION

This separation is a fundamental in creating a fear-based human culture. From the security of living with the fecund earth, one begins to live in a reality of insecurity - fear. One begins to live in a reality of conflict where militaries, hierarchs or another competing human can threaten one's survival or one's survival needs. Living in a materialistic society of accumulation, one fears to lose their possessions.

Living in a competitive society where some lose and some win, one experiences fear-based anxiety concerning their social status, their reputation and their survival income. Living in a society that is a hierarchical command system, one fears for the action of their superiors.

Living in the command hierarchy one develops the psychology of dominance/submission syndromes. In this hierarchy the slave imitates the master in order to ameliorate the conditions of their oppression. This characteristic of the psychology of the culture of empire develops obsequiousness toward authority and abuse of inferiors.

Living in a fear based society leads to a social and personal ambiance of free-floating anxiety in which the each new threat again stirs the cauldron of fear.

DEFENDING AGAINST THE FEAR - WHEN POSSESSIONS BECOME ONE'S IDENTITY

When one experiences fear, a person generally reacts with defensiveness and then anger and adrenaline gives the power to form a defense. In a materialistic society one fearfully defends their person by material accumulation. People who are fearful generally try to surround themselves with symbols of power. Big is often powerful; big vehicles, big houses, big bank accounts. In this aspect of the psychology of the culture, one usually identifies with their material possessions. One thinks of one's self in relation to one's possessions that "furnish" their identity. Possession of material objects begins to be a defense mechanism. If a modern consumer were stripped of all of their identifying possessions (including degrees, honorary titles and whatnot) it would have severe psychological impact. People subconsciously identify with their possessions. In this cauldron where people identify and defend themselves psychologically with their displays of material possessions we can see that people need to consume more in order to defend their identity. The average civilized person feels that they need more material possessions. When we multiply this by the eight billion or so people in civilization, we see one of the fundamental engines of economic growth - which ultimately comes from the earth.

CHAPTER FIVE

CREATING A CULTURE OF HUMAN POTENTIATION

CREATING CULTURAL WEALTH

We have been culturally conditioned with the image of linear increase but yet we find that straight lines and infinite growth systems are not part of earth life. Cycles and spirals are part of earth life. We have been conditioned to view our species development from "man the tool maker" in the cave to man the rocket scientist in one nice, linear, development.

Our ancient human family did not have that view. As we see in the natural world; everything cycles. The acorn is a seed pattern of future growth. The acorn sprouts and grows into a huge tree. As it reaches its point of maturation it changes from its project of assembling coherency wherein it brings in and centralizes energies of soil, sun, air and water - to its phase of incoherency, wherein it phases into disintegration as it finally dies and its parts fall off and disintegrate. At that point another acorn germinates with the whole seed pattern of the next oak tree. This pattern occurs with other species and seems to be a basic principle of biological life. This is the pre-civilized perspective where, unlike the linear perspective, the perfect seed pattern bursts and then the seed pattern matures and passes then into disintegration while another seed pattern germinates.

In the ancient tradition of the Hindus of India, the trajectory of our human species is seen to cycle through vast ages of time from the most ethereal to the most material. These ages - yugas the Hindus call them - of the species are seen to cycle and spiral. We now, they say, are in the darkest, most dense, gross vibration of matter, the Kali Yuga. We now, in addition, are at the cusp of the Kali Yuga and the cycle is turning back up toward the ethereal. This is the time that the seed pattern is set for the next cycle which will now be ascending.

It does not require reading obscure mystic documents or speaking to tribal shamans to understand that our time has come. This is a gross material cycle of which we are now at the bottom. The exploding population with increasing material consumption is hitting the wall of dwindling resources and the dying planet. This is a material society and every barrel of oil and acre of wheat can be counted. We do not need to be mystics in order to see the future. A great change is in the offing, even if we do nothing.

But we are responding. We are awakening to our human potential. Our growing inventory of resources includes the intentional community movement which has been in vigorous motion for at least forty years.(Only a portion of intentional communities are eco-villages.) In the United States the umbrella organization of many hundreds of intentional communities is the *Fellowship of Intentional Communities*. The *Federation of Egalitarian Communities* is also quite large. This is a movement that seeks to change the way we live. It seeks positive and beneficial changes in the way that we relate to each other. We have already shown the resources for our security on the earth. We have examined how we can grow food and restore the ecology of the earth. Even an emergency program has been described in which we can grow enough food for one person forever, on one thousand square feet of soil. We have shown how we can build our own shelter by hand with local materials, even to shelter that requires no outside energy for heat and cooling. You see, this is doable; we can do this. There are many examples around the country and the world where one can go look at the demonstrations of these successes.

Now that we have a rational response, a proven plan, on the ground, we can turn our attention to the people that will inhabit this scenario. Although we live in cultural poverty where humans must fit themselves into the all important mechanical, productive, apparatus and define themselves in relation to that; we can envision and create a culture of richness and a culture that promotes self and social actualization; creative personal and social manifestation. The way we raise children, the way we relate to one another, and the way we create social institutions can be changed to fit this new era. Our species has created amazing material things in this cycle but the richness of human culture has suffered because of that focus. In this next cycle of the post-industrial world, we are creating a new human culture that does not focus on the material, but focuses on the development and actualization of each human in the culture. We can create a wealthy human culture and one that serves each person. It can reflect all of the genius, creativity and growth of our species and at the same time be biologically stable, because it is not material manifestation. Truly, when we begin to raise emotionally and physically undamaged children we then will be releasing tremendous creative energy into the social body. We are creating a culture that has institutions that foster human and social development; that do not have anything to do with the gross national product.

This is an exciting prospect. This is a unique opportunity in the history of our species whose culture previously was inherited and conditioned into the masses of us. We no longer have to be confined in a culture that does not serve our needs and does not serve the needs of our planet's life. At the end of the imperial era we find that the remnants of human culture that was passed down from parent to child has almost vanished. The social bodies of the primary industrial societies are now held together administratively by laws, law enforcement type institutions and by other mass institutions over which the public has little control.

Conversely, we are taking control of our own destiny and our own development. All of the new social resources that we have created and the direction that they point is toward a human centered culture not a material centered culture.

DEALING WITH THE FEAR

As we have seen, fear is a basic reality in the culture of civilization. The herder and the farmer, unlike the forager hunters, depended on themselves and their enterprise for their existence. From that unsteady base springs anger, violence, and a continual search for security. There was always the chance of crop failure or cattle rustling.

When fear is experienced, according to medical researcher Bruce Lipton, "Blood vessels in the viscera constrict forcing blood to nourish the peripheral muscles and bones that provide protection. Fight-or-flight responses depend upon reflex behavior (hindbrain) rather than conscious reasoning (forebrain). To facilitate this process, the stress hormones constrict the forebrain's blood vessels forcing more blood to go to the hind brain in support of reflex behavior functions. Constriction of blood vessels in the gut and forebrain during a stress response respectively repress growth and conscious reasoning (intelligence)."

Fear forces people into the original reptilian brain and the primitive hindbrain.

As we have seen, the search for the psychological and emotional security that we are deprived of because of our cultural conditioning, is channeled into material consumption. People actually feel better emotionally after a satisfying trip to the shopping mall. An impressive address, an impressive vehicle, capital letters behind one's name, all help provide a sense of security. The cultural conditioning is that material things are the avenue to emotional security. This fallacy is an ingredient in the destruction of our planet.

But one needs power to live. We have the choice of the power of harmony or the power of conflict. In imperial culture with its isolation/alienation, the individual social isolate competes for survival. The means to power of the imperial patriarch has always been conflict/war. Force, destruction, death, coercion and enslavement are also useful adjectives in this case. When we look back at the first patriarch with his house, herds and fields, we see a person who is coercing and extorting the balanced ecological life for surpluses of protein. Then, we see empires that have the operative word, conquer. We see the empires militarily expand, consuming resources on the periphery. They consume soils which they begin to exploit heavily and they consume people for slaves in productive activities around the empire. Most empires had refined strategies for exploiting the newly conquered lands. The Romans established *latifundias* in conquered lands such as North Africa. Once they had the natives under control, they sorted them out and kept the slaves that would work the new project on their very same lands. The others were sent around the empire, especially to the larger cities. The Romans then would bring in "efficient" administration, the new steel bottomed plows that could plow deeply, and then they would bring in a seed inventory gathered from all around the empire, which they applied to that region to see which would produce the most. In our day, the North African ports that they shipped from, are ten and fifteen miles from the water, all filled in by erosion material and the land can hardly support goats.

"Efficiency," proper administration, increased production, are all words that beckon for a positive response from the civilized. But in fact this description is of violence and coercion. Violence and force applied to the earth and the humans. Power in this game is power to force - and death and destruction is the means to that power. Later, after North Africa became a rock pile and the forest ecosystems of Europe were laid low, science developed as a means to power. Francis Bacon who is considered an important "father" of modern empirical science explained that it was necessary to torture secrets out of the mother earth. His orientation was to force the secrets from matter.

Science became an important means to power. Science enabled, through derivative technology, the culture of civilization to refine their coercive exploitation of the earth. Farming, forestry, fishing, and many other fertility extorting activities were finely honed with new technology. We now see the results.

From a culture of fear, that divisive, conflictive and negative impulse, we are turning toward a culture of love, that unifying, cooperative and positive impulse. In the culture of empire the living flow of planetary energies are absorbed, short circuited, dammed up, and drained away from beneficial use to the living world. In our new culture, the emphasis, such as in energy medicine (massage, acupuncture, chiropractic, etc.) is on the free flow of healthy energies in the physical body. Other aspects of our new culture emphasize harmony of social relations (peace) and Permaculture certainly emphasizes increased ecological energy flows - as a state of optimum health. The focus is to eliminate blockages of energies so as to resuscitate living systems. This is power; the power to create and promote life, not the power to kill. The power to kill comes from consciousness based in panic and fear but at the end-game we find that it was not real power at all because life recedes while the patriarch sits in his fortress made of stones and dead trees with a shriveling amount of biological life left to exploit.

PROCREATING THE NEW WORLD

In a fear-based culture of free floating anxiety there is not necessarily any fear object to focus upon. The vibrations of symbols of power; conflict and struggle, reach right down into the cells of every human body. The activities of daily life are competition and struggle. Important aspects of imperial society, are symbols of death, such as video games, the adoration of "action" stars, constant violence and death displayed in the electronic media, the popularity of Humvees as family sedans, the nightly news that features the most recent invasion and mass killings; these elements are the furniture of our civilized reality. In a dog eat dog and winner take all world, the vibrations extend down to the cells and to the infants we are raising.

Many species arrange their lifestyle around the raising of the young. To life itself, the continuance of life is a major focus. A favorable place is found to raise the young, often the parents stay with the young, feeding them and teaching them so that they will have more of a chance in life. Conceiving, raising, and preparing a future for the young is the way life has had continuance on this planet. We have all been born into a dysfunctional human culture that is so fearful, isolated, estranged, and defensively self-involved that no thought is given to the future of human young. There will be no forests, fish stocks, topsoils, or even clean water to drink when they grow up but industrial civilization does not give a damn. Profits and power are the focus of the empire. Living systems are irrelevant or are simply a means to the end of profits and power if they are being exploited.

One of the most important tasks we will have in the new culture is to raise children who are undamaged, cellularly and emotionally. We are creating a new human centered culture where the frail and fragile new spirits can blossom. This means that the child bearing women receive attention.

We are indebted to medical researcher Bruce H. Lipton, Ph.D. and his colleagues who have revealed basic information about us and our cells in their research. Lipton, et. al., have revealed laboratory evidence over years of research that cells have an individual consciousness. They find that the cell membrane seems to be the focus of intelligence. In fact, the researchers have located protein molecules on the membrane that are "receptor" molecules which when stimulated by outside events, communicate with protein "effector" molecules inside, which then switch genes located on the DNA strand, on or off. (DNA is not self emergent).

Communication occurs in two ways according to the researchers. The first route is physically through the balance in the endocrine gland system (the hormones of many types whose mixture controls the physical system). These communication molecules relate to the receptor molecules. The other way that the cell receives communication is from the environment and those signals also go through the receptor molecules. These clinical discoveries have great import for Darwin's theory of evolution which says that species evolve through chance adaptive mutations in genes. Now we find that the cell monitors the environment it is in and changes itself by flipping its DNA switches to accommodate changes in its environment! This means that just like a human baby, cells can be benefitted by nurturing as well as being shut down by fear and threat.

This malleability of cells according to environmental stimuli can be shown by stem cells. Stem cells can be put into a culture of eye cells, liver cells or other cells and they develop along with and congruent with the cells of that organ. Cells are not blindly controlled by their DNA as mechanistic scientists and sociobiologists have maintained. They perceive their environment and respond accordingly.

FLIGHT OR FIGHT

The research scientists refer to the cell as exhibiting "digital" behavior. That is, the two phases of cell posture are growth and protection. Growth related behaviors of the cell, they say, are the seeking of nutrients and the moving toward life supporting stimuli. The protection response posture of the cell is to limit nutrients and move away from negative stimuli and express activities to avoid harm.

Lipton says, "Signals relaying the existence of supportive environments, those emphasizing love, *encourage the selection of growth-related genetic programs*. These decisively important love/fear signals are relayed to the fetus via the blood-borne molecules produced in response to the mother's perception of her environment. Since the offspring will spend their lives in the same or essentially the same environment as they are born in, developmental 'programming' of the neonate by the mother is of adaptive value in species survival. This is Nature's equivalent of a 'head start' program." (emphasis added)

The meaning of this is that the infant's environment sets its cellular posture and DNA switching even before birth. Thus the mother's environment; what she eats, breathes, and thinks directly effects the baby in utero. We, in mechanical society, through our researchers, are discovering how incredibly fragile and impressionable these new living beings are.

At this point there are thousands of scientific studies that show the condition of the mother to be a basic determinate to the baby's future life, even to the length of its life span and what illnesses it will have.

THE DAMAGED BABIES

An excellent source of information concerning fetal development is the book, *Tomorrow's Baby: The Art and Science of Parenting from Conception Through Infancy,* by Thomas R. Verny, M.D. and Pamela Weintraub. The authors point to one study of over one thousand expectant mothers which showed that fearful, anxious, and depressed mothers were likelier to have babies that were irritable and the more depressed the mother was the more irritable the baby. In all of the studies, premature birth and low birth rate were characteristics of stressed mothers.

The author offer a basic list of *some* of the effects of a stressed mother on the unborn:

Mothers of schizophrenic offspring are almost twice as likely to have rated themselves as depressed during the sixth or seventh month of pregnancy.

Babies with mothers under stress while pregnant are at higher risk for hyperactivity, motor problems, and attention deficits than babies of calm mothers.

Emotionally disturbed mothers give birth to babies at higher risk for sleep problems, digestive problems, and irritability.

Scientists studying the effect of stress hormones on the fetuses of rats discovered that the physiology of the brain tended to change. They found, the babies when born weighed less than average, they emitted more stress related vocalizations, and learning, memory, and growth were adversely affected throughout life.

The authors state, "Changes measured by researchers include destruction and inhibited growth of neurons and synapses in the area of the hippocampus and a decrease in the production of certain neuroreceptors. In the susceptible individual, prenatal stress causes a real rewiring of the brain, setting the stage for stress-prone reactions, from heightened irritability to behavior problems throughout life. For the child who is already genetically vulnerable, exposure to extreme prenatal stress can increase the risk for a spectrum of developmental disorders, from hyperactivity to autism."

Researchers have also begun to strongly suspect that sexuality is impacted by maternal stress. Verny and

Weintraub say that, "The precise role played by stress in human gender identity requires further study. Nonetheless, the evidence is strongly suggestive: although gender is genetically determined, the sexual circuitry of the brain, as well as sexual orientation, emerges from the interplay of genetics and environment in the womb. Of course, later influences also play a part, particularly in the area of sexuality."

THE RESOURCES IN THE NEW CULTURE

Simply having new cultural realities and living in the natural world and living in beautiful shelter that one has participated in building oneself, will affect the growth of one's life. This is real, the soil is real, food is real, the planet's life is real. It is a positive experience to be helping with this effort to manifest a mature species of humans on this planet. As they say back home, "It makes ya feel good." Beyond that, high levels of creative energy are also fun. Creativity, this is the human power. In the community life that we envision, people will be in the vicinity of the home much of the day. We will be creating new social institutions that serve us. We could easily arrange for any expectant mothers in the community to be at a designated restful place at a certain time each day where community members could come and sing, hum, om, chant, or even talk with the babies in utero. It is vitally important that these young blossoms be supported at each step of their transitions. We are focusing on living things and growing living things in this culture. This means that it must be a child centered culture. We are raising genius babies. It will be these humans who we will depend on, with their clear consciousness and creativity to lead the species with their creative ideas and novel approaches of the future. We would certainly not want to raise children whose very cells are hunched into a defensive and constrictive posture all of their lives.

Again, Verny and Weintraub point a direction. "The newest models of neuroscience tell us that sounds, rhythms, and other forms of prenatal stimulation reaching the unborn child are not merely imprinted on the brain but literally act to shape it." They also point to renowned neuroscientist Marian Diamond who has definitively shown that rats housed in enriched and varied environments produced offspring that had larger brains and were more capable of navigating complex mazes than rats not so housed.

THE BIRTH EVENT

Arthur Janov is the author of, *The Primal Scream*, originator of Primal Therapy and a researcher for many years into the psychological complexities of the birthing process. He comments on the difference between present day and previous birthing methods:

"In one of society's great paradoxes, our supposedly most advanced methods have produced the most primitive consequences, and in the most primitive societies we find the most advanced (that is, natural and beneficent) birth practice: the simple stoop-squat-deliver method. Modern technology must not interfere with the natural processes but should be used instead to aid those processes."

Joseph Chilton Pearce in his study, *Magical Child*, describes the physiological event. The contractions of the vaginal canal, he says, begins squeezing the chest so as to begin the breathing process. These contractions also massage the nerve endings in the baby's skin and awaken them. As the baby emerges, it is placed on the mother's chest where it hears the same familiar heartbeat that it has heard for nine months. Then the act occurs that Pearce says is extremely important, the mother looks into the child's eyes. She begins stroking the baby which further enlivens the nerve endings of the skin. Later, the umbilical cord is cut and the baby is pressed to the nipple. The chemistry of the mother's milk is stage specific and it changes as the baby grows through the biological stages until weaning. This sequence of actions is the basis of the bonding process between mother and child.

In the world of industrial medicine, birthing does not usually go like this. Often caesarean operations extract the baby which obviates the birthing process. This helps the mother, doctor, and hospital keep on their schedules. If the baby is birthed, it and the mother are often drugged. The drugged infant is sometimes pulled out of the mother by metal forceps. It comes into an environment that is often of a radically different temperature and the florescent light is certainly different. It is swatted to begin breathing and then laid on a metal scale. Then it is taken to a bassinet in another room. Pearce says that this series of events instructs the infant that contact with humans (the doctor and nurse along with the temperature, bright lights and metal instruments) is emotionally negative and contact with material objects (the blanket in the bassinet) is emotionally positive. As a result industrial infants often bond to the blanket in the bassinet. The phenomenon of the very young dragging around "security blankets" is familiar in our world.

Researchers have found also that industrial medicine is quick to cut the umbilical cord. This can cause anoxia, the starving of the brain of oxygen thus causing brain lesions and minor strokes. Newell Kephart, Director of the Achievement Center for Children at Purdue University says that fifteen to twenty percent of all children examined had learning and behavioral problems resulting from minor undetected brain injury caused by anoxia.

All of this amounts to damaging birth trauma. This is the industrial, mechanical society's approach to one of the most important events of living things. Janov has created a therapy that he calls Primal Therapy to deal with this problem later in life. He says:

"I have seen every possible combination and permutation of mental illness. I have seen what bad families can do, what orphanages and rejection can do, what rape and incest can do and it is still my opinion that birth and pre-birth trauma are prepotent over almost any later kind of trauma. For in that birth process is stamped the way we are going to handle our lives thereafter. Personality traits are engraved, ways of looking at the world are imprinted, attitudes are shaped. What we will become is found in the birth matrix."

Following the birth, it has been the practice in recent years to feed the baby industrial baby food (formula). As we have seen this violated the essential chemistry of the mothers milk which is stage specific for each development in the child.

Fortunately for our new culture we have resources, the skills and knowledge of midwifery has been revived. We now have many people who are able to assist the expectant mother in natural birthing and breast feeding. We have people who are even skilled in water birthing so that the baby does not come out into the air but into a warm water bath so that the shock of emergence is lessened.

It doesn't take much imagination to see that in our new culture we can create social institutions and practices that greatly facilitate this event. One of our basic tasks is to eliminate fear in the social conditioning. As we become ecologically stabilized, we also work toward the elimination of illnesses and energy blockages in the adults. This is important in that the adults raise the children and also we are working toward that human culture that is the most optimum in providing satisfying lives for everyone.

ENERGY MEDICINE

Wilhelm Reich was one of the first to draw attention to energy medicine, the focus on energy flows and blockages throughout the human body. He was a direct student of Sigmund Freud. He focused on yet another alienation, division and source of estrangement in the culture of empire.

"People who are brought up with a negative attitude toward life and sex acquire a pleasure anxiety, which is physiologically anchored in chronic muscular spasms. This neurotic pleasure anxiety is the basis on which life-negating, dictator-producing views of life are reproduced by the people themselves. It is the core of the fear of an independent, freedom-oriented way of life. The fear becomes the most significant source of strength for every form of political reaction, and for the domination of the majority of working men and women by individual persons or groups."

Reich felt that the initial damage was done by toilet training and sexual suppression. Defecation being a pleasurable act, was surrounded by guilt, prohibition, and anxiety during childhood toilet training. Sexual masturbation, touching and the ideas surrounding sex were very guilt ridden and negative. In Reich's view, the negative emotional impacts a person receives concerning these two subjects, and any others, were accompanied by spasms and cramping in the musculature. This, as time went on formed what Reich called "body armor," neurosis anchored in the musculature. This blocked energy would then emerge in negative and dysfunctional ways both psychological and in physical illness. This body armor is a basic item that energy medicine practitioners try to eliminate or minimize.

Reich felt that this was a culturally conditioned phenomenon. "Man has alienated himself from, and has grown hostile toward, life. This alienation is not of a biological but of a socio-economic origin. It is not found in the stages of human history prior to the development of patriarchy." In Reich's view the authoritarian family with its repression, especially sexually, conditioned the humans to function within the authoritarian society, the reflection. "The structuring of masses of people to be blindly obedient to authority is brought about not by natural parental love, but by the authoritarian family. The suppression of the sexuality of small children and adolescents is the chief means of producing obedience," he says.

Similar to the cell behavior when provoked by outside stimulus, Reich points to the autonomic nervous system (which relates to the inner organs) which duplicates the feat on its level. The parasympathetic aspect of this system is expansion, blood flow, elongation, and pleasure. The other aspect corresponding with the protection phase in the cell, is the sympathetic system which emphasizes fear, contraction, withdrawal of blood from the periphery, anxiety, and pain.

Reich saw civilization as an authoritarian project led by old and emotionally withered men. He worked toward an era in which the masses of people could get out from under their own built-in emotional censors and become fully alive, vital creators of their own lives. This is what Reich saw as real democracy - when the emotional plague had ended and people could act out of their natural vitality and intelligence. He says, "Genuine democracy is not a condition of 'freedom' which can be given, granted, or guaranteed to a group of people by an elected or totalitarian government. Genuine democracy is a difficult, lengthy process in which the people, socially and legally protected, have (i.e., do not 'receive') every possibility of schooling themselves in the administration of vital individual and social life and of advancing to ever better forms of living. In short, genuine democracy is not a finished development which, like some old man, now enjoys its glorious, militant past."

THE CULTURAL HOLOGRAM

We now see the contraction of the culture of empire, where it contracts ecological energy into itself. The swelling tumor body contracts all into itself in all dimensions. The contractions, even in the cells, are for the purpose of continuing the imperial project. Why do our cells contract in fear? Why do we have body armor of unresolved emotional hits? Why do the priests, politicians, and withered old men program pleasure censors into our cells? They do it to keep the tumor body growing. The purpose of the tumor body growing is to keep the emperor and his friends in the military/financial elite in power and privilege. Now, their time has come and they have run out of gas.

Now it is our time to create a viable human society out of the ashes of the failed human project of empire. We must also make the valiant attempt to redeem what to this point is a failed and suicidal human species. We can do this and we are doing this. We have created the social elements, the incipient institutions of a completely new human culture - one founded on love. We see the derivative consequences of the culture based in fear. The derivatives of love also, all fall into place. We speak the word love, which causes civilized teenage boys to snicker nervously, because this is the word and the feeling-experience. We can see how far down we are by recognizing how deprecated love, sexual love, cooperation, consideration, tolerance and all of the other derivatives are downplayed. But we must face our present conditioning. We must make love and its derivatives the centerpiece of our efforts. Love is the medicine that we need.

We are envisioning many generations living in place, on the land. We will have much time for creative cultural molding. We do need to set the foundation right and this we do by raising emotionally undamaged children. As with our ecological restoration, the institutions, traditions and practices that we establish both for ecological restoration and for restoration of healthy humans requires that we arrange our own communities in order to effect this. When we build social institutions to do this, we have built social institutions that are going to serve our own positive needs, also. When we create a culture oriented to nurturing the earth's life and nurturing babies' lives then we are going to have a culture with values, practices, traditions, ceremonies, and institutions that enrich our own lives. Many intentional communities have cultural practices that clarify communication and clarify emotions between and among people. Good honest talk among brothers and sisters can be called "transparency," "conflict resolution," or other words and many communities have worked out precise social institutions and practices to do this.

In the past decades we have developed an institution which might broadly be called "encounter group." In this group encounter, which now goes under many names, associates gather together and attempt to speak with each other honestly and attempt to clarify relations between them and to clarify their own psyche. This type of institution has become popular as a means of human contact in our cultural vacuum. This institution, in some variation, is certainly a candidate for our new culture. We have developed these resources and they can be seen in action in communities now.

Two wonderful resources that we now have to help us with issues of community are Sobonfu E.Somé and her husband Malidoma Patrice Somé. This couple are both from the Dagara tribe in West Africa. Malidoma, holds doctorate degrees from both European and U.S. universities and he and Sobonfu are initiated in their tribe. He states in his book, *Ritual: Power, Healing, and Community:*

"A true community begins in the hearts of the people involved. It is not a place of distraction but a place of being. It is not a place where you reform, but a place you go home to. Finding a home is what people in community try and accomplish. In community is possible to restore a supportive presence for one another, rather than distrust of one another or competitiveness with one another. The others in community are the reason that one feels the way one feels. The elder cannot be an elder if there is no community to make him an elder. The young boy cannot feel secure if there is no elder whose silent presence give him hope in life. The adult cannot be who he is unless there is a strong sense of presence of the other people around. This interdependency is what I call supportive presence.

"What is so good about being together with each other is that we can be the starting point for the possibility of building a larger community. Formation has to happen in a nurturing way if it is to work and prove itself to the rest of the world. In other words, it has to prove itself to be different, attractive and nurturing without the ambition of competing with the current dysfunctional communities supported by an army of policemen. And for this to happen, ritual must be constantly invoked as an opportunity for the weak to become strong and the strong to get even stronger."

Fortunately, this couple now resides in the U.S. and they are oriented toward helping us in the West develop community (through workshops and books). In her fascinating book on child raising and community, *Welcoming Spirit Home: Ancient African Teachings To Celebrate Children and Community*, she says:

"I must say that having been raised under the 'trust everyone' concept brought me many painful, although good, lessons when I first started to live in the United States. Although no one is perfect, in today's world in places where the sense of community has vanished, people too often think that humans are by nature bad, or even worse, evil. This unconscious suspicion makes it impossible for people to get close to one another- not to mention build a community. We become intolerant of others simply because they remind us too much of our own flaws. We are scared of being betrayed because we have betrayed others and have been let down too many times.

"To build community we must learn to go beyond these cultural prisons and perceptions. We must make an effort to heal our wounded self so it does not stand in our way of creating community. We can learn a great deal from the way Mother Earth holds us all - the criminals, the saints, the weak, the strong, the rich, and the poor - without rejecting us, and always giving us a chance to start over.

"The goal of community is to form a diverse body of people with common goals and empower them to embrace their own gifts, selves, and nature. Community holds a space for all its members to work at becoming as close to their true selves as possible."

When we look at the cell that has contracted in fear and defensiveness we see one half of our human nature. When we see the other phase of growth, vitality, creativity, optimism and love we see the side we want to accentuate. Growth, vitality, and optimism for the human means creativity. Few of us have had the opportunity to be released from harness and to have the latitude to be personally, socially and ecologically creative. It is a positive experience and a joyful one. Creativity is the single human power that can extricate us from our present personal, social, and planetary dilemma. Creativity is what we are cultivating. In the new culture we are formulating institutions, values, and traditions that facilitate creativity. This means that we will not be in physical and psychological harness to the productive apparatus of the emperor.

We will be free to create our own self, a human life. Our prospects are open-ended. We don't know what humans can become or are capable of. We see creative geniuses in many areas of life. They show the possibilities. We have even the idiot savants. These people, who often cannot tie their shoe strings, have one area such as mathematics or music where their abilities are so astounding, they are hard to believe. They too, show us capabilities and possibilities for the species. We are creating a human culture that has as its centerpiece the maximum flowering of each human person. This possibility is open to us now. With the dissolution of imperial culture we humans are finally left with a minimum of cultural conditioning so that we can emerge from inherited belief systems and gulp some fresh air.

SEXUAL LOVE

Sexual love is submerged in inherited belief systems. It is a power that must be controlled by priests, politicians, generals, and economic powers. If love were set free, economic powers couldn't sell products based on it. If love were free, priests couldn't threaten us with hell. If love were free no one would sign up for the military. If love were free the grasping would subside and the pleasure would increase.

We have the possibility of setting love free in our new communities. Communities of the future will no doubt be as variegated as intentional communities are now, each serving the needs of the type of members that they have, but let us continue and follow our perspective.

The ZEGG community of Germany is an example of one of the successful communities that practice free love within their society. Other groups use its variant-group marriage. Years ago when they were involved in political protest, the ZEGG people realized that the same kind of dominance/ submission dynamics were happening in their group as were happening in groups that they were opposing.

Eighty some people established a rural community and declared free love. Over three decades, this has proved stable. They have confronted what Wilhelm Reich describes as the patriarchal family and the "pleasure anxiety." They have also confronted what is rife in our own social relations. This is the power struggle of monogamy. The politics of the dominance/submission syndrome occurs with sexual partners in this society. Questions of ownership arise and questions of emotional dependence arise. These things are minimized when love is free.

When love and its experimentation are free for the youth, they can devote their great energies to creative pursuits rather than molding their lives around the elaborate courting games of finding and catching the "one true love," the idea so beloved by the Victorians.

When we have a wealthy culture, we will have created social institutions to help the youth discover and learn the most basic treasures of life. Love is free and we can have it in abundance but we must have cultural traditions and institutions to cultivate this deeper love and regard.

LIBERATING HUMAN ENERGY

We see the basic pattern of human action - protection or growth. Protection means conserving and contracting energy into the interior in preparation for the big fight. Growth of course does not mean the shallow and superficial concept of the materialists. Growth means human growth, the growth of human potential, alive to the cosmos. Many people have had the experience of the aliveness, of being involved in a creative project. Especially as children, before we became routinized, we had this exhilarating experience. This creative energy is our power and pleasure.

In civilized society we are conditioned into patterns so that our energy is channeled into the productive process or the administrative and social processes that facilitate the productive process. We plod along and are mentally alert to the questions of, "Is this the right way to do this?" "Is this the way the authorities want it done?" "What rewards will result if I do this right?" or maybe, "If I don't do this right what will happen to me?" We scramble and compete but it is for foreordained goals.

When we civilized, with our dominance/submission syndromes, are put in a situation of true freedom, for example with a group of people who want to achieve a goal but there is no authority and no set prescription of how to do it, we are usually initially confused. Most of our lives and a big share of our days are taken up with doing things that are prescribed for us by someone else or some mass institution. We are not accustomed to looking at the big picture and creating a course of action among ourselves. We are not accustomed to the creation of a dialog with a group of people, defining a goal and then creating a plan of action toward that goal.

That circumstance will change. We stand on the edge of an explosion of great creative energy. We stand on the precipice and are handed the problem. The problem is that the human species, as its special kind of organism, has reached a cul de sac. The end game is here. Who we are, what we do in our daily life and the life of our society is suddenly obsolescent. A massive, corpulent human society has exhausted its fuel and stares into the abyss.

This is our liberation, whether we are deciding where the refugee column should make camp or whether we are banding together as a group to populate a watershed, we will be making our own group decisions and creating our own direction. This is the liberation of our creative energy that will become the future. Far from being a tragic event, the end of industrial civilization is our liberation.

GOOD GOVERNMENT

Politics is power and force in the culture of empire. The pie is divided up and the constituents struggle for the biggest pieces. Fertility and materials are coaxed up out of the earth and the struggle begins, to determine who will get what share. This is conflict management. Great material accumulations exist that require managers and policy decisions, power. This is the nature of power in a mass, materialistic society. In a forager/hunter group there is power, the power to endure. In a cooperative foraging group a big item of group discussion might be where next to move camp or where the harvest is ripe and the game fat. The elders are listened to but there is no coercive authority. Forager/hunters do not have police or jails. That is not their culture. They flow with the current of ecological energy through their terrain. Items that come to the level of "politics" are rare with them.

Civilized people tend to look at a "chief" the same way they look at generals or presidents. These in fact are not analogous. Some anthropologists (Pierre Clastres, prominent among them) view the forager/hunter tribe as a political arrangement that deliberately controls centralized power. Here you have a human group in which no one controls any individual's food and shelter supply. Each has the knowledge to get their own. Within the definitions of the empire there is little power to struggle for. By creating an institution of spokesperson, headwoman, headman, or "chief" they have created an institution without power as it is defined by the empire. Normally in tribes the spokesperson does not have command, coercive power over anyone. Contrarily, when a war chief is selected, all concerned follow that persons direction for the duration of the hostilities whereupon the function of that office ceases.

People who share the most are the most respected in this culture. Thus, the poorest people are often the most respected. This exists with the chief who is expected to share greatly. Some tribes actually allow the chief position extra wives. Women are the power in tribal society. They produce the food, clothing, raise the children and really do much of the meaningful "work" in society. Thus, if the tribe places a number of wives with the chief, there is more to share because of the productive power of the women. It should be noted that female tribal leaders are well known in tribal society. One does not necessarily have to be male to be a chief in many tribal groups.

There is a role for this tribal leader; it is as peacemaker, orator and visionary. The everyday orations of tribal leaders are often recitations of oral literature, usually having a cautionary moral. The chief is respected and because the chief is usually old and wise, the chief's words are heeded.

THE NEW POLITICS

A new resource has emerged out of the body politic that we can use. It is called consensus politics. Many organizations now use this method as do many intentional communities. It is essentially based on the concept that everyone in the group must agree with a decision before it is implemented. This is grassroots democracy. In industrial, parliamentary democracy one elects another to represent them. There are the levels of local, county, state, nation, U.N., and then more rarified groups that have power over us such as the World Trade Organization. At each succeeding level our control is diluted and the ability of the elite to insert itself in the power equation (usually through money) is increased until we come to something like the World Bank or the World Trade Organization that are powerful institutions but we know little about them and have even less control over them.

Consensus politics has a framework and procedures but these are much less complex than the Roberts Rules of Order that is usually used as a framework for local parliamentary democracy. When we have been on our watersheds for several generations and we have achieved a population in line with the carrying capacity of the land and we are self-sufficient, there will not be much materialistic or military power to struggle for or debate. This is the point. If there are a lot of materialistic goodies and power over others to struggle for, there is much politics. If the effort of the culture is to be creative, happy and free, there is no focus of struggle.

Caroline Estes, a leader in the Alpha Farm intentional community is one of the most prominent teachers of consensus political procedures. She has taught workshops around the U.S. and the world for several decades. She demonstrates to groups who are not yet using consensus politics that we have a real and valuable resource in the procedures for consensus politics that enable groups to formulate, discuss and agree on matters more quickly, smoothly and satisfactorily that many had thought possible. It is a wonderful tool for our kind of needs. In keeping with our new cultural perspective, it tends toward agreement of all. When the U.S. government tried to get the Hopi nation to adopt parliamentary democracy (in the form of a Bureau of Indian Affairs sponsored, Tribal Council) they rejected it. Their feeling was that they had gone along for a thousand years with their consensus government where all agreed to a decision and why should they abandon that for a system in which fifty one percent win and forty nine percent are aggrieved and forced to accept?

THE POLITICS OF LOVE

We can see the pattern here. The equation is fear, scarcity and struggle on one side and love, cooperation, and abundance on the other. We can see that the politics of empire culture springs out of the basic soil of its patterns of separation, selfishness, and survival fear. The patriarch practices politics of centralization and control. The spoiled child, possessed by fear, kicks and screams on the floor in its strategy to control the adults around it. If the child or the patriarch can establish control their survival anxiety will lessen.

The politics of love describes a strategy of agreement. Pushy, desperate, neurotic, and fear based people often succeed in the politics of conflict but they stick out like a sore thumb in politics of agreement. The politics of love is a politics of nurturing. We will be living in small communities, nurturing the ecology and nurturing human community. Our political discussions will be how best we can cooperate together to achieve the nurturing.

THE CURRENCY OF LIFE

In our present world, money is at the base of the survival desperation; but we are headed for a new world where new things will become important and new "values" will appear.

Now, the banker friends of the emperor are empowered to loan out money that they don't have. That is for every dollar that they have in the vault they can loan out ten dollars. This, among the elite, is called fractional banking. Thus, the ten dollars that they loan out contains a nine dollar fraction that was created out of thin air - and the borrower has to pay back the entire ten - with interest to the emperor's friend, the banker!

In that different type of world, which we are creating, what is of value is entirely different. Instead of a rich economy and a poverty stricken human culture, we are creating a rich and varied human culture that has only peripheral use of currency. We know of two complex societies that did not use money, the ancient Egyptians and the Inca of South America. Certainly small communities could manage this.

But nonetheless, the new institutions have already been created - if in case we do feel we need to go beyond sharing the harvest and need some monetary form of barter exchange. This happens when local people decide that they need a more satisfactory form of currency. They band together and create their own. Most of the many hundreds of local currencies around the world travel under the banner of LETS systems. That stands for Local Exchange Trading System or Local Employment and Trading System. In many of these local economies the members create money themselves. If a carpenter comes to do work for a plumber, the plumber gives her a LETS script for one hour or whatever the value of the work is agreed on. The carpenter then has a script that she can spend with the plumber or the baker, or the candlestick maker. This, then, initiates the local currency as others join in. It is free; it is not controlled by the emperors bankers and it allows transactions and economic flow to occur through trading that could not occur if the two parties were broke (did not have the coin of the emperor). The hundreds of LETS systems functioning all over the world demonstrate another facet of the new culture that we have already created.

THE LANGUAGE OF LOVE

We, who are the life of the earth are increasing our Being. Our nature as humans allows us to amplify and potentiate what now lies dormant, waiting to unfold. Like the unused capacity of our brains, there are other potential abilities that can be cultivated. The clarity and strength of our communication is one of those. Communication is conscious relationship and also energy relationship. Communication at a telepathic level with the other beings we live with will amplify the experience of life. This is a distinct possibility of future cultural creation. The planetary life has put humans, whales, dolphins and elephants in one similar niche. They have great ability to form images and to communicate them. Because of the fold of the frontal lobes of the brain, we species are particularly suited toward complex communication. The little we know about interspecies communication in forager/hunter culture suggests that communication with other species enjoys a long tradition.

Communication between humans on a verbal level uses the tool of language. Language reflects the focus of attention of the culture. In the language of the Inuit of the far north is said there are more than thirty descriptive words for snow, its different conditions. In the ancient language of the Greeks there were many descriptive words for love, the various qualities of its manifestation. Language - semantics, carries the culture and becomes a tool of thought with which to think in that culture's thought forms. In that respect, as we learn languages we learn the cultural nuances. In creating a new cultural form we need create new language appropriate to that cultural perception.

We find that in English as well as many other languages of civilization there is much confusion. In many cases similar sounds mean different things, different word sounds mean the same thing. Language, as we know it, is indistinct. To add to this we are now coming into the age of double-speak in which elites employ psychological operations and media manipulation teams to confuse and disinform the masses.

An example of the type of linguistic pattern that we need has been discovered by John W. Weilgart, which he describes in his volume, *aUI: The Language of Space*. He had a thorough background in linguistics, psychology, and philosophy, but created this language through a visionary revelation. In this revelation the seed ideas of a new type of human language occurred to him. "aUI" is the name of this language. It is not the type of language that we are accustomed to. Abstract symbols like letters do not denote or connote meanings. Instead there are a set of thirty-one basic symbols that reflect the basic intuitive realities of our existence. These are such things as space, movement, light, human, life, time, matter, sound, feeling, round, equal, inside, quantity, quality, and so forth. Out of these basic categories thoughts are put together intuitively and analogically. The symbols for each of these categories is congruent with their meaning such that "inside" is a circle with a dot inside of it. Feeling is a heart shaped symbol and active is a lightening shaped symbol. Next, Weilgart created the sounds for each symbol so that the sound is intuitively similar to the meaning such that the sound for inside is a guttural sound coming from deep inside the throat. The way that the thoughts are combined can be shown by the abstract thought-meaning-symbol-sound: anticipation. In aUI this becomes fore-feeling and it uses the heart symbol for feeling with the symbol for before in front of it. Weilgart has also created a sign language in which the arms and upper torso form the symbols. This provides an additional level of congruence of meaning for each symbol.

Dr. Richard S. Hanson, Professor of Ancient Near Eastern Languages at Harvard University says that:

"In discovering aUI, Prof. Weilgart had discovered something of the nature of language in its primitive state and something essential about human communication at its beginning stages. This ‘language of space’ is not a concocted language like esperanto. It is a rediscovery of the basic categories of human thought and expression.

"To semantic theorists this should be most interesting. By working with basic categories of meaning and a simple set of aural and visual symbols for each, Prof. Weilgart has succeeded in making language definitive rather than merely denotive or conative. Basic categories are communicated through single symbols and new concepts are created by merely combining the basic symbols by way of a simple, intuitive logic. The result is language which has the simplicity of archaic speech plus the sophistication of modern thought."

There are a number of cultures known to modern anthropology that use several languages within the culture. Among the Apaches of Southern New Mexico there existed a "war language" that was only used in expeditions of war. Among other cultures there are known to have been spiritual languages, used primarily for discourse on spiritual subjects. Certainly with the creation of new culture the need for new language exists. The languages of empire carry all of those definitions of reality within it. If we use a pure language that has no emotional connotations connected with it, we will be greatly aided in creating new social reality.

aUI is so intuitive and simple that Weilgart was able to teach it to many different groups. Individuals of these diverse groups such as military servicemen, children of tribal societies, and U.S. school children were able to begin communicating in the language within a few minutes. Weilgart, among other talents, was a professor of Psychology. In this capacity he used this language to facilitate communication with people classed as schizophrenic. These people, who ordinarily experience confusion in communication, were able to improve their communication significantly because of the precision and clarity of the language that they learned after a brief introduction.

SPIRITUAL LOVE

The mystery of our existence in the cosmos and of the mystery of the existence of the cosmos itself is addressed by religion and spirituality. The mystery remained a mystery with our ancient human family. In many tribal groups, spiritual energy simply emerged in some people. People would say that this person has "medicine" to heal one certain affliction and another person might be said to have "medicine" to cure some other affliction.

Geronimo, of the Southern Apaches in the late eighteen hundreds was one of the leaders of a band of twenty-eight people that were chased for five years by up to one quarter of the U.S. Army. Nana, an old man in his eighties rode with them. He had "medicine" for finding military wagon trains full of ammunition. Lozen, a renown woman warrior who rode with them had "medicine" for finding the enemy. She would stand on a high location and while chanting would twirl around in a circle. According to the tingling in her arms and hands she would point to the direction of the imperial invaders and according to the redness of her hands she could determine how close they were. These are examples of some non-healing types of "medicine" people might have.

Tribal shamans enter other dimensions of consciousness, sometimes with the aid of psycho-active plants. This often aids them in gaining information for cures and for future direction for the group. In some tribes there were hereditary medicine people but others also developed "medicine" for certain things. The practice of spirituality was rather democratic in forager/hunter cultures.

When the inversion into patriarchy and agriculture occurred this changed to a matter of control and centralization. As a mirror of the culture, hierarchies of power and expertise developed in imperial religion. These hierarchies of social power which had captured the spirituality of the masses were normally under control of the emperor and the elite. Religion became an extension of state power.

One means to power of the empire is human intellect. It is the intellectual function of the human that has been salient in the empire. Among the various functions such as emotions, contemplation, intuition, spiritual revelation and others, intellect has enabled the growth of empire to the recent historical era of science and technology. We would expect this to be reflected in other areas of the culture and we do find it in the mass hierarchies of imperial religion. Religiosity in the empire functions from the intellect with many libraries of books, memorized doctrines and heated philosophical debates called theology. These are also religious dictatorships. The patriarchs who control these politico-religious organizations in the West are mirrored by the "Gurus" of the East. Both East and West are consistent in their "escape" orientations. The Guru patriarchs of the East promise escape from the horror of material existence through awakening into other dimensions of consciousness. The patriarchs of the West promise "escape" from the horrors of materiality into heaven. This escapist tendency is entirely consistent with the basic pattern of separation, alienation and estrangement patterned into the rest of the culture.

We have now entered an era of new spirituality. Intuitively, out of the population have sprung many new directions in spirituality. The motif of the new emerging human culture is an amazing tolerance concerning the spiritual beliefs and practices of all involved. Earlier, in the patriarchy, religion and its proselytizers followed the sword of state imperial power. Now as the new culture emerges we see a great tolerance. In the last four decades there has been a great flowering of interest in spirituality among people who are culturally creative. Shamanism, psychedelia, psycho-cybernetics, Hawaiian Kahuna practices, past life regressions via hypnotherapy, psychic development training, paganism, magic, wicca, and many more avenues of interest have developed. A characteristic of this new interest is an insistence on direct experience rather than words, rituals or theories. This variety and richness is our new culture in terms of spirituality. This is a new culture of spiritual freedom in which each actualizes their own spirituality.

Recently an inversion of the Eastern Guru patriarch has developed in the U.S.. This breakthrough has occurred with Saniel Bonder and the group called Waking Down in Mutuality (.org). In this model, which reflects the pattern of freedom of the new culture, the emphasis is on deepening the conscious manifestation into materiality (thus waking down rather than the earlier waking up and out), being here on the planet earth in full consciousness. The people associated with Bonder are manifesting a new phase, a new cycle, of completely conscious material embodiment of the species. This is the perspective of the Waking Down in Mutuality teaching; to more refine our ability to be in materiality; to advance the project that we came here to do.

Bonder assists other people to achieve expanded states of consciousness. These people then help others as the energy spreads. These people do not maintain a command hierarchy. They do maintain a functional hierarchy of the awakened assisting the newcomers. Their social form and relationships is a horizontal mutuality. As new people are attracted to the group they are aided by mutual assistance. There appears to be an understanding with this group that far from dealing with sky gods who wear white and float around on clouds above us, what they are dealing with is a natural psycho-physical development of the consciousness of the organism.

Our new culture, as it emerges, appears to be pointed toward a new direction for the species. The intuitive manifestations of cultural direction by cultural creatives is going toward self actualization and species actualization.

OUR WAY OF LIFE IS A GRADUATION INTO A NEW WORLD

Humans are a very resilient species. They can be starved, beaten, threatened for long periods of time, raised in terrible environments, fed bad food, provided polluted air to breathe, and many other kinds of abuse, yet they are still standing on their feet. These kinds of conditions exist for many of the species now on the earth and people are able to endure it and keep going. In the centers of the industrial empire people exist in a poverty stricken culture where they manifest heroic effort in order to maintain their material display. Long hours of work, long hours of commuting, little time for family life, teeth grinding competition, and obsequiousness toward superiors characterize those who achieve success in the materialistic world of the shopping mall culture. In many ways, except for the material circumstance, one could be a slave in Babylon or Rome. It is true, the will to survive can carry us through terrible conditions of life.

But we are not discussing endurance, we are pointing to a completely and qualitatively different reality. We have now an opportunity to create a human culture that not only allows us simply to endure but to thrive in ways even the most affluent present society cannot. Each one of us have tremendous creative abilities. We are now coming to a time in which our energies can be directed toward creating things that are basic and fundamental to us. No longer will we direct our life energies to things that are perfunctory and required. In our review of birth and development, we have seen how fragile the blossoming of a human life of quality is. This is akin to the creation of beauty. By group effort we can achieve a place of beauty in which to live and we can create an ambiance of beauty and we can raise children that are beautiful and undamaged. We are creating a way of life that provides healthy water, food, air, habitation, and social environment for children and adults.

With group effort we can put ourselves on Mother Earth in a way that can revivify the earth and does not exceed the carrying capacity. As we continue to pursue our creative culture we will devise new and potentiative ways to relate to one another. A consciously created, land based, human culture, one whose purpose is to serve the needs of the individuals involved and potentiate their possibilities is a new development on the earth. By taking charge of our own life, by taking charge of our community life, and by being responsible to the earth, we will be generating a new human Being on earth, in a culture of love.

ABOUT THE AUTHOR

Author Wm. H. Kötke is widely traveled and published. His most recent book, prior to *Planet Garden*, was the underground classic, *The Final Empire: The Collapse of Civilization and the Seed of the Future*.

He has been a journalist, a radio script writer, a pamphleteer, a novelist, an essayist, and has had many articles published in periodicals.

With a background as ranch hand, sawmill worker, labor organizer, a Bachelor of Arts degree, wilderness resident, activist with the Native American resistance, and resident of the Jicarilla Apache and Navajo reservations, Kötke has the depth of education and experience to flesh out theories with living examples.

Printed in the United States
92543LV00004B/10-57/A